STOLEN CHILDHOODS

Stories of Estonian children deported to Siberia

Helle-Liis Help, Toomas Kodres, Olvi Kuusik, Kaljo Käspre, Leo Lipre, Ants Lond, Märt Lond, Rita Metsis, Vello Ojaveski, Allan Onton, Ivi Peekmann, Karin Rammulus, Rein Saluvere, Hilmo Seppel, Aime Tootsi, Malle Vesilind

Translated by Kristiina Paul
Edited by Peep Aarne Vesilind

LAKESHORE PRESS

In memory of our parents
who were, with us,
deported to Siberia

Let this collection remind us of our unforgettable youth – friendship, love, the irresistible desire to become educated despite the seemingly insurmountable obstacles – and how we overcame that which was taken from us on 25 March 1949.

TABLE OF CONTENTS

FOREWORD

EPILOG

Many of our friends have already left us. We bow our heads in memory of fellow authors Karin Rammulus and Kaljo Käspre and also commemorate all those companions in fate who started to write their stories but did not have time to finish them before they passed on: Õilme Vilder, Ipe Kabin, Oskar Niitepõld, Endel Rammulus, and Harri Teever.

The Estonian Children of Krasnoyarsk

Foreword

On 25 March 2009 the Estonian people commemorated the 60th anniversary of the deportation to Siberia of 22,061 Estonian men, women, and children. The ceremony was held at the Museum of the Occupations and was organized by the Government and the Parliament of the Republic, with President Toomas Hendrik Ilves as the main speaker.

On that day the Estonians who as children had been deported in 1949 and who had settled and studied in the town of Krasnoyarsk in Siberia once again gathered for their annual reunion. As always, they enjoyed the reunion and each other, reminisced about the times past, inquired after the children and grandchildren, and in some cases also great-grandchildren.

But there was also a surprise. Allan Onton, without whose organization these reunions would have been less frequent, presented a proposition. He suggested that each person write down their life stories, including a description of their lives before the deportation and what happened once they came back to Estonia. The proposition received a positive response but nobody knew what would become of it.

Four years later the sixteen long-awaited stories were collected in a booklet that the authors shared with one another. But then the participants began to consider the possibility of publishing a more permanent book that detailed their experiences – one that would be more readily accessible to a wider audience. This required a translation, and Kristiina Paul, an Estonian living in Canada, was asked to translate the stories into English. Estonian-American Peep Aarne Vesilind was asked to edit the manuscript and to publish the book through Lakeshore Press.

This book records the stolen childhoods, as told in their own words, of the Estonian children of Krasnoyarsk.

Bath, NH, USA
2014

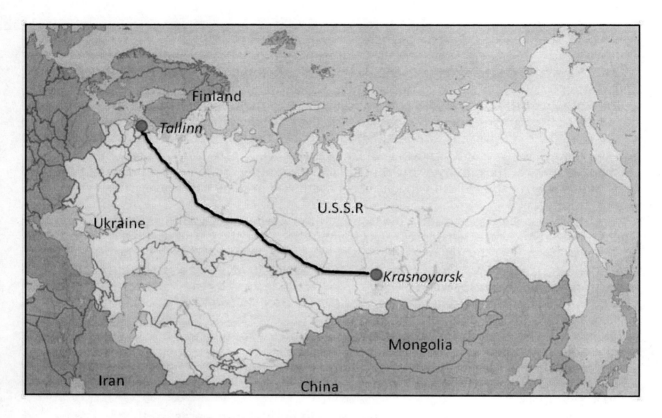

From Tallinn to Krasnoyarsk to Tallinn

The authors gather at Malle Vesilind's home in Pirita, summer of 2013.

1. Ants Lond
2. Dagmar Lipre
3. Leo Lipre
4. Toomas Kodres
5. Rein Saluvere
6. Vello Ojaveski
7. Malle Vesilind
8. Märt Lond
9. Aime Tootsi
10. Olvi Kuusik
11. Helle-Liis Help
12. Rein Tootsi
13. Ivi Peekmann
14. Hilmo Seppel
15. Rita Metsis
Missing: Allan Onton
Deceased: Kaljo Käspre and Karin Rammulus

STOLEN CHILDHOODS

Stories of Estonian children
deported to Siberia

Chapter 1

Leo Lipre

I was born on 19 July 1928 in Tallinn. Father Peeter was a government official at the railway of the Estonian Republic and Mother Alide (nee Kull) was a housewife. The roots of Father's family tree reach Poland and Lithuania (Grandfather George) and East Prussia (Grandmother Ottilde). Grandfather was a railway construction foreman for the Tsar's rail and that brought him to Rakvere and Kunda and left him in independent Estonia. Grandma Ottilde who was German by nationality was in 1946 at the age of 70 deported by the Soviets to Ufa region and the location of her grave is unknown.

Mother's roots are in a south Estonian family Kull. She was one of 12 children. Great-grandfather Prints' and Great-grandmother Lota's graves with stone crosses have been preserved at Tõrva cemetery. My best guess is that I am 50% Estonian, 25% German and 25% Polish.

In 1935 we moved from Heina Street in Pelgulinna to Virve Street in Järve. My school life started at the French School in 1936. I remember my classmates Helmut Rosenvald (composer), desk mate Albert Norak (finance minister of ESSR[1] and mayor of Tallinn), Eino Baskin (actor) and many others. The closing of the French School in 1940 took me and Helmut to Elementary School No. 8 and from there to Gustav Adolf Grammar School (GAG) in 1942.

Sister Kiira (1927) went to Tallinn Girls' Grammar School No. 1. She was the liaison for our GAG boys' class for arranging mutual initiatives with girls of her school.

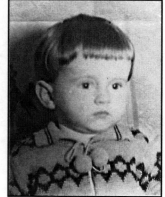

My time of studying at GAG (1942-1947), despite its relatively short duration, was most memorable, and the boys in my class established contacts that have lasted throughout their lives. The background of war, life struggles, and other inexplicable events have cultivated a sense of togetherness, responsibility, and desire to learn. Class reunions still take place every year on the first day of school, 26 October.

First portrait, 1929.

---

[1] Estonian Soviet Socialist Republic [Ed.]

Our family, 1932.

During GAG days I took part in many things: listening to birdsong with the ornithology club, building a radio, raising rabbits, frequent chess games at the chess club, and of course the weekly sports competitions that as a rule ended with a dance party or other school parties. Orchestras would play at the dance parties. Many schools had their own bands but the best band in those days was our GAG's "Mickey." They continued playing together for many years after they had all graduated. I also remember the dance parties at Erich Kõlar's "Kuldne 7" (The Golden 7). The school parties were proper and fights were rare.

Fench School field trip, 1937. I am in the front row, third from left. To my left is A. Norak. E. Baskin is first on left, back row.

The peculiarity of class breaks was the gathering of school friends around the music class piano where Peeter Rekkaro, Felix Mandre or Olaf Jürme would play pop songs of the time. School violence was unknown.

Even though the lessons were short during the war (25 to 30 minutes) we were, as life has proven, sufficiently educated. The teachers were in most part pedagogues with great experience and effective teaching style. They shared the characteristic of not inciting negative emotions in students. Of the 28 graduates of our class, seven earned their doctorates in sciences and one even became an academician.

With benchmate Elmar-Ants Valdmann (1928-2005). At GAG graduation, 1947.

Most of the boys in our class went to Tartu University in the fall of 1947. I, together with Kalju Hallik and Hans Ilves, took the admission exams to the Department of Civil Engineering at the Tallinn Polytechnic Institute. I did not finish this program because of my unexpected trip to Siberia.

For more than twenty years Father participated in the rail workers' mixed choir "Raudam," and for a long time he was the choir senior and the assistant to the conductor Karl Leinus. That kind of "socially dangerous" activity led to Father's arrest in 1945 as a bourgeois nationalist.

On the eve of deportation on 24 March 1949, Mother was anxious – she had heard of an approaching deportation to Siberia and she insisted that we should not spend the night at home. My mother went to her sister's house in the next street. I stayed a few houses over at my friend Uno Tölpus' place, and my sister stayed with her boyfriend Artur.

In the morning of 25 March Uno's mother went outside and said everything was peaceful at our house but that that there was a truck parked at the other end of the street. Uno and I got ready to go to the lectures when I discovered that I had left a notebook at home. I went to get it and then...

Our house at Virve St. 1 had an attic. Half of downstairs was a grocery store and the other half was our apartment. The upstairs had two apartments. When I opened the front door I was shocked. There were four or five people in the hallway. Would running away have saved me? I calmly continued on, as if I were going to the second floor. I was politely given way to pass at the landing but I had barely made a few steps upwards when one of the comrades followed me and demanded an ID. He then demanded that I open the apartment door.

For almost an hour I sat in the dining room with the gang of deporters.[2] Nothing was happening. I suddenly noticed the front door handle slowly moving down. I was frozen with fear. One of the men rushed to the door and found Mother behind it. Mother said she didn't know where her daughter was.

---

[2] The deporters were groups of four to six men, communists or communist sympathizers, who were assigned to arrest certain people and to take them to the deportation trains. They were mostly Estonians, most likely with an armed NKVD agent in charge.[Ed.]

The deporters now became active and vocal. They read out loud some old document signed by Molotov about forcible exile and we were told to start packing. We were given two hours to get our things together. Mother told me we should only take what we would be able to carry ourselves. We packed two mugs, two spoons, two knives, etc. Meanwhile they had found out where my sister was and with their truck had been to Toompea where she worked with my uncle at the planning committee. We now made a correction: we took three mugs, three spoons, etc. We took only the necessary clothing, but one of the deporters, a man who spoke Russian, took the potato sack Mother had brought and started stuffing the contents of the wardrobe in it. *Vam prigaditsa*, (you will need it), he said. Our belated thanks to that man!

Transport to the railroad station was "a car in front and a car behind." We rode in a very large pre-war truck Büssing NAG. It was a sunny day, the unseasonally fresh snow sparkling. We drove to Aruküla where they had parked the train that was headed for Siberia, out of sight from the people of Tallinn. We lifted our things from the truck into the cargo car. The soldiers who surrounded the train allowed us to leave the car to bring back *kipyatok* (boiled drinking water).

The cargo car had the "typical furnishings": two-level bunk beds at each end and a tin stove (*burzhuika*) in the middle. A hole in the car floor surrounded by cloth walls was the toilet.

There were longer and shorter stops on the way to Siberia. The trip took a couple of weeks. We were only allowed to leave the car to bring *kipyatok*. I'm surprised that I don't remember what food we were given.

For our family, the rail trip ended in Nazorov in Krasnoyarsk territory. State farm trucks drove in front of the cars on a railway branch, bags were off-loaded, and the trip continued through the roadless steppe, along muddy and broken spring trails.

The Adadym state farm was gigantic, with five departments. We were taken to the Second Department where fifteen Estonians were housed along with some locals. There were some "apartments" consisting of open kitchens.

Our "hostess" was a divorced woman with a daughter. She was the Communist Party organizer at the state farm. Five of us lived in a 20 square meter room that included a stove-oven. The unpainted wooden floor was always very clean because the daughter scraped it with a knife. I often wonder how our "hostess" must have felt when we were told to move in with her.

At the spring plowing and the subsequent seeding I operated the devices pulled behind the tractor: three sets of plows or five seeders (the area the covered was about 15-20 square meters). Steppe fields are not comparable to fields in Estonia. They are massive, often being a kilometer or more in length.

After the spring work ended I was assigned to digging silo wells. I liked this work, and I still enjoy digging (if I now only had the strength). During haymaking I was paired with a Kalmyk. The entire nation of Kalmyk had been sent from the banks of the Caspian Sea to Siberia.[3] He was a bigger and stronger man than I, but he was also a slowpoke and often impudent.

---

[3] Kalmykia is the only Buddhist region in Europe. Kalmykians were badly persecuted by the Bolsheviks after the revolution and as result during the Second World War were active in assisting the invading German army. After the war, in retribution, Stalin ordered the entire nation of Kalmykia deported and

4

A positive memory of the life on the farm was the steppe in the spring with its small tulips and other colorful flowers, as well as late night gatherings of Estonian youths in the canteen (where my mother was the cook). We sometimes even had dancing and music. The local children (and possibly others) frequently gathered at the window to watch. I guess we were different!

Half a year later, in the fall, our family was deported again 500 kilometers further north to Angara, even though harvesting had just started and the state farm was short of workers.

When we were all ready in the truck, about ten older local women came to see us off, some with tears in their eyes. *Gospodi, na sever*! (God, to the North!)

In hindsight, that deportation turned out to be the lucky break of my life.

We were first taken to the "distribution center" at the edge of the city of Krasnoyarsk where we lived without anything to do for a couple of weeks. Then one early morning we were put on a towable barge. The trip along Yenissei River went downstream, about 300 kilometers to the mouth of the Angara river (the width of the river is eight kilometers at that spot!) and then to a new barge upstream along Angara. We traveled for 130 kilometers to Motygino harbor village where we were put ashore.

From Motyhgino we were taken another 30 kilometers on a truck to Razdolnoye, in the Udereisk district of Krasnoyarsk territory. Razdolnoye was a mono-settlement in the middle of the *taiga*,[4] established for the purpose of mining the precious metal antimony ore. It's a remarkable place, located just 80-100 kilometers south of the impact area of the famous Tunguska meteorite.

A couple of days later the "slave market" took place – that's what we called the distributing of the arrivals to their jobs. At a long table sat the representatives of the departments of the mine: recruiters from mining, forest factory, capital works, communal economy, etc. One by one people were called to this committee and they learned who could do what. When I had presented my credentials (second year student of the civil engineering program), one man immediately said, *"Etot moi tšelovek"* (This is my person) and I was assigned to the technical department of the capital works department (OKC). My sister was sent to planning, so we ended up working in the same

Our first "house" in Siberia.
The house had no roof and no door.

<hr />

dispersed to Siberia. Today Kalmykia exists as an autonomous region in the Russian Federation but only 11% of the population is Kalmykian. [Ed.]

[4] *Taiga* is a dense, northern forest consisting mostly of pines, spruce, birch, and latch trees.[Ed.]

building. In the technical department I was involved in drafting of construction graphs and project archives. My boss was Viktor Sergeyevitch Medvedyev, an engineer-scientist of airplane hangars. He had been repressed in 1937 during the purges and he treated me in a fatherly manner. (He visited us in Estonia in 1960 and was ecstatic about the Nõmme garden city.)

A year later I moved from office work to the position of the foreman for the painters, and soon I was the technician in the construction department (assistant to the foreman who later became the manager at the mine.) I would spend one winter in the warm underground, supervising the concrete work of the pump house (Outdoor temperatures of -40°C were quite common in the winter).

We were living in the stables, a big room about 10 meters wide, furnished in three rows with bunkbeds and tin stoves. With my mother's participation we bought a small semi-detached house together with the Jürise couple. Viira Ants came to rent with us.

We were in close contact with the Estonians, celebrated each other's birthdays, and participated in my friend Ants' wedding. On Saturday evenings we often went to dance at the club. I also fondly remember a Polish girl and a Ukrainian one.

My sister's husband, Artur Vaikjärv from Estonia, visited us in the summers (school holidays). Because of these visits, he was almost expelled from the Young Communist League, which would have meant the loss of his Stalin-scholarship. The decision of the student committee to strip him of his membership was fortunately not approved. The Russians decided that "ljubov jest ljubov" (love is love).

Self-taught engineer at the mine, which was 170 m deep.

Ants and Helle-Mai wedding.

Half of this house was ours. I had also built the summer room at the left.

6

Grandfather with his daughter's son Kalju Vaikjärv. The other little boy belongs to Ants Viira.

My sister and her husband Artur Vaikjärv in 1951.

In 1951 writer Herta Laipaik and daughter came to visit her deported husband, surgeon Nikolai. He was my longtime chess partner.

After graduating from the Tallinn Polytechnic Institute, Artur had himself transferred to Razdolnoye and as a free man worked as the chief economist of the forestry factory. Their son Kalju was born in Siberia.

We received newspapers from Estonia. News also came by way of writer Herta Laipaik, who came to visit her deported husband, a surgeon at the local hospital. Herta Laipaik wrote the novel *By Angara Anno 1950* (Tallinn, 1991) about life in Razdolnoye. It is a work of fiction but the characters, including our family, appear with their own names.

When my father got out of the Altai prison, he came as a free man to Razdolnoye to his family and got a job as a warehouse worker for the canteen. Mother went to the commandant's to fight for justice: she demanded passports for us as we had been deported because of Father who was now free. A couple of months later Father was called to the commandant's office and his passport was taken away.

After Stalin's death (1953) it became easier for the young deportees to get into schools. The only way to get a residency permit to the city of Krasnoyarsk was to go study (or to pretend to study).

View of the Razdolnoye living area from the mountain.
Here I lived from 1949 to 1954.

The project group of the construction department, most of whom I knew, were Russian engineers repressed in the 1937-1938 purges. They had been relocated from Razdolnoye to Krasnoyarsk. They recommended I come and work with them in Krasnoyarsk, at the building planning office known as OTB-1 (Osoboje Tehnitcheskoje Bjuroo, later Sibtsvetmetprojekt).

For a residency permit I had to apply to the Construction Technical School (1954) because I was afraid that I might not be accepted at the Construction Department of the Siberian Institute of Forest Technology.[5] My career in construction, which lasted for 60 years, started with the job at the OTB-1.

For two years I had listened to lectures at the Tallinn Polytechnic Institute and that became the basis for self-study and practice. I must say I was in good company. The nonferrous metallurgy factories that were designed there were massive by Estonian standards, and their construction was complicated (multi-leveled and for big loads and with openings in the bulkheads). I am still surprised my older colleagues trusted me with this responsibility and allowed me opportunities for professional development.

Having arrived in Krasnoyarsk, I was facing residence problems. I spent the first night at the technical school. After that I found shelter with a nice elderly Estonian lady who had a free bed because her daughter had been sent to a collective farm for a month. The

---

[5] The name of this institute, translated verbatim from Russian, is "Siberian Technical Institute of Forest." Because of the awkwardness of the translation, in this book the institute is referred to as the "Siberian Institute of Forest Technology." [Ed.]

8

recommendation came from my future brother-in-law who on his Tallinn-Krasnoyarsk travels had made the aquaintance of the family.

The owner of the bed turned out to be Dagmar, who was sent home from the collective farm prematurely because she had had her fingers caught in the hatch of the grain truck. I had to find a new place to live.

I rented a room at a detached house close to work (a typical village house with blue shutters). At first my mother was worried about how her little boy would survive by himself and came to cook for me, but she returned to her own place after she and my father found out about Dagmar Treikelder. We were married in 1955 and were given a room in a three-bedroom apartment. Dagmar became the comptroller at a big grain factory.

Dagmar and I honeymooned in Razdolnojes Village.

Dagmar (1929), together with her mother and brother Peet, had been sent into exile to the Kirov region for the first time in 1941, had returned to Estonia, and had then been deported for the second time in 1949. Their father, a successful businessman, had escaped to Sweden in 1940, but their mother had refused to leave. Dagmar's mother suffered greatly during those years. After she returned to Tallinn from the 1941 deportation, she was put in jail for three years and then in 1949 again deported to Siberia, along with her daughter and son.

A gradual liberation of the deported began in 1956. Sister Kiira was the first to be set free as her husband Artur was a "free" citizen. Next came the older people, including my mother and father. When Dagmar and I received our passports we decided to stay for another six months because we needed money. We both were earning decent salaries.

Having arrived in Estonia in 1957, I went to work at the Estonian Industrial Project (then ESSR Design and Research Institute of Oil Shale) as senior engineer of the construction department. I received the industrial-civil construction engineer's diploma in 1961.

Our first residence in Estonia was in Kivimäe where, with our own hands, we had built a small apartment in the former storeroom of my aunt's house. During that time our son Toomas was born. Daughter Katrin was born in 1964 when we were already living in our private home in Maarjamäe.

I worked at the Industrial Project for 35 years, as a senior engineer, team leader, chief engineer of a sector, and director of Construction Department No. 1. The last 10 years I worked in the management of the institute as the deputy chief engineer and director of production. The main task was communicating with the planning committees of the republics of the Soviet Union and distributing work and salary funds among different subdivisions of the institute. There were about 200 employees.

Controlled economy was mandated; free enterprise led to jail. Even a highly regarded academician like Endel Lippmaa had difficulty understanding the strictness of the controlled economy. One day he came to my office (communicating with clients was my job) and requested that we immediately start planning a biocenter in Tartu. He said that he had received approval for this project from high offices. I explained that it would not be possible to do this, that the banks had to give us approval for any project and that such approval would be difficult to obtain. He was very upset, but this was the Soviet system.

One of the active members of the "Community of Krasnoyarsk Siberians," Allan Onton, worked at the Industrial Project for a long time. He was one of the best project chief engineers I had. The projects he led were always completed on time and within budget.

In those years we had no hope of ever being released from the grip of the Soviet Union. I had planned early on that once I reached retirement age (60) I would give up working (I would retain 70% of my salary) and that we would live at Maarjamäe in winter and Hiiumaa in summer, where I had in 1980 purchased Nurme Farm in Pühalepa Parish.

In 1987 during *perestroika* some departments, including the Building Committee, were given permission to start small companies (basically private companies) in their area of expertise. These companies were not given state-planned jobs and made their income from private contracts. My retirement age arrived in 1988 but contrary to my earlier plans I decided to test myself as an entrepreneur.

Director of Construction Department No. 1 giving a speech.

10

A small company, T-Projekt, a subsidiary of Industrial Project, was born. It was the first design company of its kind in ESSR. I convinced Uno Martinson (project lead engineer at Industrial Project) who had also reached retirement age to join me. I also taught young Anu Kaminski to work as our technician-draughtsman. The three of us worked full-time and eight to ten specialists from the Industrial Project worked part-time on contracts for different parts of larger projects.

T-Projekt did very well, for several reasons. One reason was that, after a few accidents with metal buildings, the Building Committee allowed only our buildings to be constructed at state institutions. The state institutions could not take on these jobs if the client could not provide the design work, so we almost had a monopoly. We had many job offers and a lot of money. We were handing out bonuses to the Industrial Project, to the management, to the planning department, to the cleaners, and to the security guards.

Estonia was on the path to success. In 1993 the Soviet-era small businesses underwent compulsory liquidation. Uno and I reorganized T-Projekt into two companies; I ended up with Projekt TL, Uno with V-Projekt.

Now, in the days of my retirement, making DVDs of our trips has become the most time-consuming hobby. It's not at all tiring, however. Exactly the opposite: memories give you an emotional charge. The bad thing is that puttering around the house and in the yard is becoming secondary.

Children's and grandchildren's successful lives provide great satisfaction and joy in my old age. Son Toomas graduated from Tallinn Polytechnic Institute, a civil engineer (takes after his father, successful construction entrepreneur); daughter Katrin graduated from TPI from the accounting department (took after her mother) and is now a civil servant. There are four grandchildren. Both have a son and a daughter (they take after their father and mother). The grandchildren have been very rewarding and great fun.

When I was young I dreamed about how nice it would be to live to be 70 and see the new millennium – 2000! Now I'm working on 85 and life is filled with pleasant memories! Next to my family, fellowship with my friends and travel companions has always been important. They have helped and they still help maintain the zest for life.

Chapter 2

Helle-Liis Help

I was born on 3 September 1934 as the fifth child to the family of the attorney Rudolf Kuuskmaa and homemaker Anna-Marie Kuuskmaa (née Lauba).

My carefree childhood years, until the beginning of the war, were spent in Pirita. In August 1941, during the first Soviet occupation, our brand new home in Pirita, in the current location of the lifeguard station, was torched. We moved in with my grandfather at Metsavahi Road 11 in Pirita. In 1942 I entered the Practice School of the Tallinn Teacher's Seminary.

When the Soviet Army returned in 1944, my father, who was the director of a nationalized printing shop in Lühike Jalg Street (formerly Roosileht & Co. Printing House where Father had been shareholder), was arrested. Three copies of an anti-Soviet flier (one of which was found in Saaremaa) had apparently been reproduced with their printing press. Thirteen people were punished for this.

On 25 March 1949 a window at Grandfather's house was broken and armed men stormed in. We were given an hour and a half to pack. There were four of us - my mother (47), brother Hillar (22), sister Maie-Anne (19), and me (14). Older brother Endel (25), who had married and lived elsewhere, was spared. The communist security troops looked for him everywhere. Endel was about to turn himself in, when one of our relatives, Vello Sillam, convinced him to hide. For the next few weeks Sillam hid Endel in a small room that he had been renting.

After being driven to the railway station at Ülemiste, we were herded into a cattle car. There were 25 adults and 15 children in the wagon. The journey started at noon, and during the second night we crossed the border to Russia. There was no toilet in the cattle car and we did not get any food until the third day when we were allowed to buy some loaves of freshly baked white bread.

After a fortnight of travel, at the Archinsky train station, some of the cars were disconnected but we continued on. More cars were disconnected at other stations the next day. Finally, ten of the 45 original cars arrived at the final destination of Uzhur where we disembarked.

We were put into three open trucks and began our 180 km journey. The road was in very poor condition and muddy and the surrounding landscape bleak. Every truck had a guard who was supposed to be our "guardian angel," but ours barely allowed us to move. Several times the truck got stuck in the mud and the rough ride caused many of us to become carsick.

The first people were unloaded at a fairly prosperous *sovkhoz*[1] where they even had electricity. We, along with four other families, were taken to a *kolkhoz* farm in the Kalyažikha village near Daursk. We arrived at night. The chairman of the collective farm gave us a warm welcome – tea, milk, honey and bread were on the table. We spent the night at the *kolkhoz* farm office.

Two days later the farm commandant collected all of our passports as a precaution against possible escape attempts. We were given one kilogram of beef per person, eight kilograms of rye flour and 20 kilograms of potatoes.

Two houses were set aside for the five families – one with a single room, another with two rooms. We got the two-room house for three families (eight people). In the beginning we had to sleep on the floor, but then we brought in birch boughs from the woods and the men crafted beds for us. Our first jobs were logging and road work. We also dug a garden around our house and planted vegetables.

Mother, sister, and my extended "family" in Kalyažikha, 1950 – calf "Miku" and pig "Ats," who came when called by name.

Mother, who had finished Elfriede Lender's Girls High School, and brother Hillar, who had escaped from the Soviet POW camp in Varkuta, knew Russian. I had had no chance to learn Russian and this became a severe problem for me. When school started in the fall, I hoped to enroll in the seventh grade. I was, however rejected by the Daursk Secondary School because I did not speak Russian. In addition, it was too hard to walk the ten kilometers to the school every morning and then ten kilometers back home at the end of the day. As a result, I began attending grade 4 classes at the local elementary school just so I could learn Russian.

I also learned that we had to address our teacher as Klavdiya Aleksandrovna, not just Klavdiya. This shocked the entire class. [2]

The following year I attended secondary school and lived with a Russian family from whom I rented a kitchen table and a cot below the ceiling in the same room. I got along well with

---

[1] A *sovkhoz is* was a state-owned farm. A *kolkhoz*, on the other hand, was "owned" by the workers. The *sovkhoz* employees were paid regulated wages, whereas the remuneration system in a *kolkhoz* relied on cooperative-style distribution of farm earnings. [Ed.]
[2] Estonians did not use patronyms when addressing someone like a teacher. "Aleksandrovna" means "daughter of Aleksander." [Ed.]

14

the family, but was nevertheless too shy to ask for some big potatoes that the hostess boiled for the pigs. People in Russia don't eat unpeeled boiled potatoes, yet I would have very much liked some hot potatoes.

I continued to have a problem with language, such as in the first chemistry class – what does *probirka* mean? [3]

I had three "3s" on my report card the first quarter[4] but the homeroom teacher still gave me a thin, blank sketch book as a gift for "good progress in studies" (these books were in short supply in those days, just like blank white paper). I had no "3s" on the report card by the end of the year.

Occasionally my brother Hillar also roomed with the same family. He was the hostess's

The Forestry Institute sports team. I am first on the right.

favorite and was given a bed in the big room. He slept on a bag of feathers under a feather blanket.

I later stayed with Evald Mägi, engineer, retired Soviet Army captain, and brother of Hjalmar Mägi, our physics teacher, and his wife, the dentist Magda Mägi. Their home had a pleasant atmosphere.

The first medal – gold medal – graduate of the Daursk Secondary School was the Estonian Enn Luisk (son of a dentist). The next medalists were in 1954 – from my class. Valeriy Vlassov received the gold medal and continued his studies at Moscow University. Leonid Dukatchov and I were both awarded the silver medal.

I forwarded my documents and qualifications to the Krasnoyarsk Forestry Institute in hope of studying wood hydrolysis (the process of making ethyl alcohol from wood). Their response was positive.

I had been promised a room in the student dormitory but when I arrived this did not materialize. An official at the institute, a pleasant young lady, thought that I probably wasn't given the room in the dormitory because of my status as a *spetsposelenka*.[5] Fortunately, I was temporarily taken in by total strangers, Estonians who lived in a small apartment. After that I went to live with the kind family of the youngest daughter of family Mägi, Ingrid, where I shared the room with the newlywed couple, while Ingrid's mother-in-law lived in the kitchen.

The Baltic students were a tight group; there were many parties with a lot of singing. Girls were lucky because there were more boys than girls. My studies went well and I was in the upper quarter of my class.

---

[3] Test tube. [Ed.]

[4] Her grade was 3 out of 5 where 5 is best. 1 to 5 is the common grading scale in most of Europe.[Ed.]

[5] Literally, "special deportee," but defined as "deported without court order." Once someone had been deported they carried the stigma for the rest of their life. The institute did not want to get into political trouble by giving dorm space to a deportee. [Ed.]

Father was released from prison in 1953 and found a job as an accountant in the Estonian SSR. He was very concerned for his family and sent us money when he could.

In 1955 I received the news that because I was a student, I could return to my homeland. It turned out later that our entire family could go home, thanks to Father and Hillar, both of whom worked hard to obtain the necessary permissions and documents. We began our journey home on 12 June 1955 and arrived five days later.

Many good people greeted us at our arrival even though it was raining cats and dogs (which seemed a bad omen). Their welcome demonstrated to us again just how selfless and generous our relatives really were.

Hillar, Maie-Anne and I found a home with our Aunt Anna (Father Rudolf's sister) in her one-room apartment where she lived with her husband Uncle Hans.

Mother and Father were promised a home in Aurküla with Father's niece Linda and her husband Arnold Viira but that never happened because a month later, on 20 August, our father Rudolf Kuuskmaa passed away at his work desk. He had worked so hard on our behalf and everything had gone according to his wishes, but now his stressed heart just gave up. The funeral expenses were covered by the cartel where Father had worked as an accountant.

All four of us, his children, managed to get back to our studies at the Tallinn Polytechnic Institute (TPI). I started my studies with the second year of chemistry in the mining department. Brother Hillar was reinstated into the second year of the same department, and sister Maie began the first year. Oldest brother Endel was back for his last year and now all four of us were university students at the same time, even though the age difference between Endel and me was eleven years.

I graduated from TPI in 1959 as an engineer-chemist-technologist and was directed to the position of engineer at the Chemistry Institute of the Academy of Sciences (salaried at 88 rubles a month).

On 23 December of the same year I married Kalju Help. The wedding ceremony took place at Vastseliina church on the second day of Christmas, 26 December. Wedding receptions were held both in Tallinn and at Kalju's home at Päevakese, Võrumaa.[6]

For the wedding of his little sister, Hillar supplied two cases of vodka. (Later he also provided two cases of vodka for the wedding of his older sister.) All other expenses were taken care of by Kalju, who had been employed since 1952. He had also, during his spare time, been preparing to defend a thesis for the technology candidate degree.

For the wedding, Kalju's wonderful relatives installed electricity in their home and the party was great. The bride and her relatives from northern Estonia were surprised by the love and talent for singing of the Võru people. Everyone knew by heart the words to the songs.

In 1960 I was transferred to the Oil Shale Institute and moved in with my husband to Kohtla-Järve. Our son Toomas was born on 29 August 1961. In 1963 when Kalju was already employed as the chief specialist of chemistry and oil shale at the Coordination Committee of Scientific Research (CCSR), we moved to Tallinn. In the same year Kalju was asked to teach at the Tallinn Polytechnic Institute, and I took his position as the CCSR's oil shale chief specialist. This was a scarily high position; my big supporter had been Katrin Karisma's mother, my colleague Niina Karisma, who has worked as the chief technologist at the Järvakandi Factory.

---

[6] Võrumaa is a county in the southernmost part of Estonia. [Ed.]

After CCRS activities ended in 1964 I worked as an engineer at the Construction Bureau of the Ministry of Local Industry on Pirita Road. Twins Helen and Andre were born on 19 February 1971. In order to spend more time with the children at our summer house at Vääna-Jõesuu I began working as a teacher in 1972. The same year we took a trip to the USA at the invitation of our cousin, Andu Lauba.

In 1979 I was invited to work as the scientific secretary of the Coordination Committee of Scientific Works of the Estonian Academy of Sciences. I am currently working at the Academy, now as the editor of the Estonian publications of the Scientific Information Department (strange, considering my Russian secondary education). I like my work and communication with erudite people and find it very interesting.

Looking back I remember with gratitude many good people that life has brought me together with, but especially my mother who worked so hard in raising her children, and who, even after the difficult years spent in Siberia, set an example with her warm heart and infinite compassion. When she died at the age of 91, the ribbon on her wreath read, "Rest in peace, noble soul!"

Chapter 3

Vello Ojaveski

I, Vello Ojaveski, arrived in this world on 18 August 1934. Place of birth was Antsurahva farm in Harju county, former Kõnnu (now Kuusalu) parish in Vihasoo village near Loksa.[1]

The owner of the farm was my father Rein, second eldest of my grandparents' seven sons. He became the owner because the oldest son, Ludvig, refused to have anything to do with the farm and took a job in the city, being at first employed there as a city official and later advancing to the position of mayor of Tallinn-Nõmme.[2]

Before the First World War and during the Communist Revolution my father had lived in Simbirsk in Siberia and witnessed what the Reds did there. What he had seen probably contributed to his death in 1941.[3]

Father Rein actually had the education of a sailor, having graduated from Käsmu Sea School, and having taken part in the War of Independence in the Peipsi[4] fleet of the nascent Estonian Navy. He had no special calling to farm work but stayed to work the farm when he married Hilda Reskov of the neighboring farm. Their firstborn son, Toivo, was born in 1931.

My life has in part progressed in parallel to Toivo's (childhood) but also in unexpected chance meetings (in Siberia), and of late as fellow citizens and co-owners of our father's farm that was returned to us after Estonia regained its independence. Our sister unfortunately died as an infant.

Our childhood was safe, and the relations in our family and with our neighbors were good. Noteworthy was the creation and legalization of the joint resting place (a unique cemetery) on the high bank of the Loobu River for the departed people of our and the neighboring Pauna farm.

Our childhood ended with the occupation of Estonia in 1944. In the beginning of November Father was called someplace (presumably to the Loksa boatyard or the parish administration) and was arrested. Father had worked at the docks, which were considered to be of military

---

[1] Loksa is a small town on the Gulf of Finland, east of Tallinn. [Ed.]
[2] His story is archived in the Nõmme museum, located in the Nõmme Station building.
[3] The year the Soviets first invaded Estonia. [Ed.]
[4] Lake Peipsi forms part of the eastern border of Estonia and separates Estonia from Russia.[Ed.]

importance. Men were being arrested for many reasons, including resistance to the formation of collective farms.

Father was first taken to the Nõmme militia station and from there to Patarei[5] prison in Tallinn. Mother took food parcels for him there. When no more parcels were accepted by the prison, she started to wonder what had happened to him. Finally a letter arrived and it turned out that he had been taken to Crimea (!) and from there through "one sixth of the world" to the far east, Magadan. He died there in June of 1946.

Brother Toivo's and my paths parted on 25 March 1949. It was the last day of the spring break. In the morning, Mother came to our room and said that there were rumors in the village – people were being deported. We were not worried because we knew that this had nothing to do with us. The next morning Toivo went to Tallinn to school and I went to school in Loksa. I think it was after the second or third period that a boy ran upstairs to the classroom and said that they came to get me.

I went downstairs. Mother was there and told me to gather my things, that we were being deported. I remained very calm. The school's principal, Arn Mikiver, wrote me a note stating that I was a sixth-grader. It was very poorly and nervously written. We were taken to the yard of the Russian military garrison next to the school, where trucks with loads of stuff and people were already waiting. We didn't know anyone on the trucks except for Aunt Kamilla.

Soon the trip to Kehra station began. When we drove past the school, the entire school was looking out of the windows at the people who were leaving. I have later thought that I could have waved goodbye, but everyone was in a trance. I was later told that there were no more lessons that day; the teachers came to the classroom, but they just stood by the windows and looked out. Everyone was silent.

In Kehra we were stuffed into cattle cars. Mother and I were among strangers. Aunt Kamilla was in a different car.

The journey started at night. Windows and doors of the cattle cars were tightly closed. The window shutters were opened only after we had arrived in Leningrad.

This was already four to five years after the war, yet the surroundings of Leningrad still showed the effects of the war: demolished wagons, burned houses, forests of trees shorn off with half-trunks still standing. After Leningrad began Russia's boring monotonous scenery: swamps, bogs, birch brush, muddy roads (mud gutters), gray villages and filthy railroad towns. When we reached the Ural Mountains we were allowed to open the doors. There was nowhere to escape to now!

Every now and then we were given some sloppy soup. To satisfy one's natural needs there were several opportunities; a barrel in the middle of the rail car was used by the women and the open car door by the men. When the train stopped, everyone rushed out to do their business under the car and behind it – men, women, and children all together. The trip lasted about two weeks, including long stops. When our train started heading south from the Atchinsk station, it was a great relief. Son station was the last one.

The train stopped on the side of a high mountain, and the station was down below. All the baggage and people poured out of the train and rolled down the hill – some somersaulting, some running, some skipping.

There was a large closed yard below where we were all gathered. It looked like a slave market! Here the directors of collective and state farms picked a workforce for themselves.

---

[5] Patarei Prison was a notorious military garrison prison in Tallinn. It is now a museum. [Ed.]

Families with men were valued. Men who knew farm work were in demand. But there were many elderly people and children. These were distributed evenly among the farms. [6]

We drove about 70-80 kilometers at night, and upon arrival were stuffed into an empty house.

In the morning we got an overview of our whereabouts. Many houses were without roofs. During the war, the roofs had been burned for heat. There were one-room log houses with ovens in the middle; some were just boards in some kind of ruin. The village was surrounded by flattish mountains with a few higher and rockier ones in the mix. We soon took a sightseeing trip to the top of one of them. Estonians named that one "the devil's mountain," as it was always kind of grim with black clouds coming unexpectedly from behind it.

Next we were again divided. Mother and I were housed with a widow who had a son the same age as me, a bit younger daughter and a newborn. Our corner of the room was shared by an older man and woman with their daughter from south Estonia. Within a couple of years everyone in that family had died.

Sometime later we moved into a house with two other families – a small square log house with two windows but without a roof. When it rained we had to put buckets everywhere.

Otto Liinmaa from Tallinn and his mother lived with us. Otto had attended the Pedagogical Institute and was an English philologist – a smart man but with a bit of an unbalanced nervous system. He worked hard but started to drink. When he returned to Estonia, his mind was all messed up.

With us were also Ants Räägel and his mother, probably from Abja. This man looked like my father, but he had the mannerisms of Kaval-Ants[7] and he got along very well with the Russians. There was also a girl by the name of Männipalu from Kasispea who had lived in Tallinn at the time of deportation. I think her first name was Vaike. Most of the Estonians were from south Estonia: from Abja, Kilingi-Nõmme and Abja-Paluoja. The Soobiks had a large family – many children. The husband became a blacksmith at the collective farm. There was Kaask with his wife and daughter. The husband was a tractor driver and died in an accident.

There was also a man by the name of Peeter with his wife and son. I don't remember their last name. The man spoke a bit of German and the only Russian he knew was what sounded like *pochemu*,[8] which he said all the time. He first asked a question in Estonian and then added

---

[6] Brother Toivo, when he was in the Red Army in Russia, once went to such a slave market and talked to the farm directors. Apparently they had been told that a group of "German sympathizers" were being brought in and that they could choose whomever they wanted. Some shied away from this, fearing getting trouble-makers, but others gladly chose the deportees to work on their farms. The farm director he was talking to had not chosen any of them and regretted his decision. Apparently these deportees were great workers and most were even "cultured" (they were literate). Mother told us how the local women had admired the Estonian women's underwear. They had apparently never seen such clothes. Estonian women often fed their families during the early days of their exile by selling their clothes for food.

[7] "Clever-Ants," a children's story character who knew how to get his way by schmoozing up to everyone. [Ed.]

[8] *Pochemu* is Russian for a person who is a nuisance because he asks too many questions. [Ed.]

pochemu.[9] And then the others had to translate. He was a very interesting person, a bit of a philosopher with a perpetual smile.

On the third day everyone was sent to work. It was time for the spring seeding and the tractors were very busy. I was put to carrying grain to the field with horses. The fields were large, up to 40 hectares and with black soil. There was no need to fertilize – manure was carried out of the barn and that's where it stayed. Mushrooms grew on top of the manure piles. Estonians picked and ate them as the Russians watched in amazement.

We had had to sign a paper every week to prove we were still there but later we had to sign only every month.

During the spring seeding I was made to walk in front of the tractor with a lantern to show the way because the tractor had no lights.

Soon the hay season started. At first the tall steppe grass of the previous year was cut, and when the young grass was tall enough, that too was cut. Estonians worked in their own brigade, piling up the hay and then having a woman stomp on it to pack it tight. The Russians, on the other hand, piled the hay up with wooden pitchforks and did not stomp on it, because the amount of work done was measured by the height of the pile.

When people went to use the hay in the wintertime, the Estonians' hay pile contained good hay. It took effort to find the Russians' pile under the snow, because it had collapsed and turned black. Only then was the Estonians' labor appreciated. It was like that with all jobs. The Russians did their jobs haphazardly, but the Estonians were used to doing theirs properly. The Russians kept wondering how the Estonians could do all kinds of farm work. When an old Estonian woman could write her signature, there were already comments: she's educated, probably a schoolteacher! When Russian women received a letter from a son in the army or from a relative, they often came to the Estonian women and asked, "Read it to me, because I can't."

In the fall all Estonian children went to the first grade of the village school. There was one young teacher for the entire school. The next day I was taken to the second grade and on the third day straight to the fourth grade. There were no higher grades. That's where my education continued. At first it was difficult, especially the Russian grammar. I must admit that the teacher treated us very kindly and with understanding. In the other schools during my education it was the same thing – a very understanding attitude towards us Estonians.

In the spring we walked about ten kilometers to another collective farm to take our final exam. There lived one of my mother's girlfriends from her youth with her husband. Her nickname was Meika. She constantly smoked and didn't work, and was entirely dependent on her husband. Her husband was later an accountant.

The next summer during haymaking I was the hooker on a tractor. In the fall I herded horses; all day long I rode around in the steppe and sang songs.

That fall I went to the next village to study in grade five. Initially I lived with an old woman but soon moved in with the Mõistliks. They had their own house and were a nice family. I attended school with Eerik, the older brother. Huubert probably rode the tractor, and there was another young man – I don't remember his name. Eerik's mother was very kind; she cooked

---

[9] It is unclear why Peeter was saying *pochemu*. Perhaps he meant to say *ponimaesh* which means, roughly, "Do you understand?" [Ed.]

and was very caring. There was another boy, Enn Kivi, who lived at the collective farm where I had gone to take the exam.

One day the collective farm's postman came to get me and told me to pack my things. "You're leaving because your mother is being transferred," he said. Mother spoke Russian well, and I guess she had convinced the commandant that we should be allowed to go elsewhere.

We were taken to Horse Breeding State Farm No. 42, named after Budyonny.[10] Mother ended up in a department called the Gate. It was situated high among the mountains, which explains the name. I, however, went on to a state farm center 25 kilometers away, because there was a school there with seven grades.

At the farm center I found a family of Estonians who took me in. Mari and Juhan Tilla with their three sons of my age, Enn, Jaan and Juku, were from south Estonia. Mari was a seamstress and Juhan worked at the sawmill. I also worked at the sawmill in the summer. We carried logs from the Yenisei River and rafted them down the various branches of the river to an easier place to pull them out. It was generally a good life – no worries.

In the winter I went back to school. The teachers were also nice. I especially liked the physics and math teacher, Konstantin Leontyevich. The communist authorities had not considered him trustworthy because he had intelligent parents. He was strict, proper and with a keen sense of humor. We treated each other with respect. There was also a former pilot, the school's principal, who taught us German. His German knowledge, however, was even worse than mine. When he was reading new text, he would questioningly look at me and was pleased when I nodded in approval.

The winters were cold, minus 30-40 degrees C, but that was manageable because we had warm clothes and valenki.[11]

I got well acquainted with a Russian signalman who lived at his sister's, next to the Tillas. He was a former seaman, a good accordion player and a hunter. I often sat with him, listening to his songs and stories from his military service in the Far East. For a short while he had even worked for the Yankees on a mother ship at auxiliary services. Most of his stories and songs were of women and hunting. He bought me a 26-caliber single-barrel hunting rifle. I often took it to the mountains in order to chase ducks on the swampy lakes in spring and fall. My entire bounty was one deer, three or four ducks and... many misses. In the summer we built houses using railway ties. We broke rock in the mountains and transported sand and gravel. We did all kinds of construction work.

There were many Estonians at the state farm. The most conspicuous was Talts, a real Mephisto. He was strong, with an erect beard, long front teeth and high eyebrows. He was despised by the Tilla old man, because he would always grab the better and more lucrative jobs. He was the first one to build himself a house. Another Estonian was Hendrik, a bachelor and a despiser of women. He did all kinds of construction work and was a man of jokes.

There was an old man from the Abja area whose name I don't remember but who was legendary. He wore a long sheepskin coat. On his feet he wore shoes made of car tires. He was bearded and rather grubby. He ate very little and was a miser, but the word was that he had loads of money. Where he got it or where he kept it, no one knew. When the state farm had cash flow problems, however, they borrowed money from this old man.

---

[10] Semyon Bodyonny was a cavalry officer and a crony of Stalin. [Ed.]
[11] Heavy waterproof boots, traditional in Russia. [Ed.]

We also played sports in the summer, mostly volleyball. In the summer of 1952 the district sports party took place where there were many kinds of events, from horseback riding, to motorbike racing up the mountain, to track and field. We came in second in volleyball, but I won the 100 meters, long jump and high jump. I was also among the winners at shotput. The awards ceremony was like this: a name was called, something was randomly selected from a big cardboard box and it was put in your hand. I don't remember everything but I received a pack of *Armeiskyie*[12] cigarettes, a pair of socks, perfume, etc. This experience was what prompted me to go to the Physical Education Technical School in Krasnoyarsk.

I wrote a letter to the commandant's office and waited for a reply. There was not much time left to take the trip and the exams, but the permit was not coming. Then the commandant came to the state farm and said that he'd left the permit at the district office. I jumped on my bike and rushed the 50 kilometers there. When I got there I was told that the permit had been taken to the state farm. I rushed back. When I got home I was told that the permit was taken away since I had not been there. I got back on the bike. I finally

With Toomas (on my left) at the Krasnoyarsk Railroad Workers' Club.

received the permit and went home.

The next day I traveled to Krasnoyarsk. The technical school was situated in an old brick building on the city's main prospectus named after Stalin. The toilet was outside. Admission was simple – a few physical exercises and an exam on the Soviet constitution. This took place as follows: everyone picked a ticket they liked, prepared their answer and then went to see a hung-over teacher and briefly told him about the topic on the ticket. With that,

Party at Karin's parents' place in Zaozjornaja.

---

[12] *Armeiskyie* was a popular brand of cigarettes during the Soviet time. [Ed.]

you were accepted.

When school started in the fall, I discovered one more Estonian. That was Harri Teever. We immediately became great friends. He had already finished the first year but had lost his place at the dorm due to some row in which he had not even been at fault.

He slept by putting a few chairs between two beds and covered himself with his big fur coat. However, I think he still received a scholarship. Together we spent the money my mother sent, and that's how the two of us lived for two years. I realized this only later, but then everything was great and natural – everything must be shared.

In the second year Toomas Kodres joined us and now there were three of us. Three girls also came – Silvi, Lia and one other. But they could not handle the work and left.

In the winter of the second year my brother Toivo, along with many Estonian boys who had been conscripted into the Red Army, were assigned by pure chance to Krasnoyarsk. Together we attended parties in the city and in the summers sunbathed along the Yenissei River.

Many Estonian young people had come to Krasnoyarsk to study. We communicated with Hilmo Seppel, Endel Rammulus, Karin, Õilme, Rein, Peeter and the others. There were many men and women let out of prison camps but left in exile who lived and worked in the city. Among them I found (or rather Harri found) Ain Paartalu, a man from our village. We had gatherings at the Estonians' places, with Õilme or Karin's families. We sang, had drinks, and spent time in a merry way. The biggest crowd of Estonians was together on the last New Year's Eve, in 1956 – in a half-built radio and TV factory. I didn't know many of them but it was all one family.

During my last summer there I met another man with an interesting fate. He had come from the north and had been sent from the mines to practice sports in Krasnoyarsk. He had a lot of money and therefore we had many adventures. He had attended a German military school in Czechoslovakia and later served in Tallinn, and who knows where else. At the end of the war he had been sentenced to death by the Germans due to a row with a German officer, but a psychiatrist he knew had declared him crazy and he'd escaped. He had then hid in the forest. When the Russians came, he had tried to make it across the Gulf of Finland in a boat. But he was caught on the beach and again sentenced to death.

The sentence was changed to 25+5[13] years, as was common. The year after I came home he also was set free, with all rights. I met him in Tallinn where he wanted to buy a car at the market. Of course he couldn't do that. He went to Moscow and from there he was supposed to go to his wife who was living in Latvia.

Winters in Krasnoyarsk were perfect for skiing. My skis had been made at the Tallinn Ski Factory. Sometimes it was just too cold to ski and thus I did not practice that sport very often.

The last summer there was especially great. We went swimming and sunbathing at the Yenissei and also prepared for the final exams.

Before the exams I asked the principal how I could be directed to work in Estonia, because by then I was already a free man. He said that this could be done if I wrote to Moscow and asked for permission. But the problem was that I wasn't a member of the Young Communist League. I quickly joined and mailed the letter. The response from Moscow was that they had no objections; let the local directions committee decide. The local committee also didn't object to my wanting to go to Estonia. I later heard that there had been a plan to send me to the Far East to work as a teacher at the children's colony under the Ministry of Interior. Ouch!

---

[13] Common designation in the USSR meaning 25 years in prison plus 5 years in exile.[Ed.]

After graduating I immediately went home to Mother. We packed our stuff and... goodbye to Siberia!

From the Achinsk station we took the Far East train on the way to Moscow. This trip was pleasant. It was August and the weather was nice. Home got closer and closer.

In Moscow we had to spend the night in the Leningrad station. I walked around in the station and was wondering about the station life - the entire floor was covered by sleeping people. The cleaners came at night, went to one corner, woke up the people and washed the corner. That's how they worked the entire enormous hall, and people were peacefully moving from the unwashed parts of the floor to the washed ones. The next day we got on the train and the trip continued. It was a wonderful feeling to see Estonian villages again after passing through Petseri. The most surprising was Tallinn where the majority of the people spoke Estonian but I did not know any of them. How unusual!

Mother and I first went to Poula's (uncle Ludvig's wife Pouliine) and agreed that we would stay with her. I got a job at school No. 27 in Rahuäe. This was one of the most negative experiences in my life so far. I had learned everything only in Russian. Here I had to step in front of a class and use all the terminology in Estonian. The classes were big, and boys and girls were together. Tiki, the school principal, was a very strict and pedantic pedagogue. He didn't curse at anyone but he sure could make one's life hell. At every staff meeting women were crying because of him. I lasted for half a year, but then I'd reached my limit. The pay was also poor. I guess I had become a disruptive influence, because I was fired, along with a man by the name of Külaots. I found a job at the Ship Repair Factory organizing physical activity at the workplace.

When I told Kalju Ojaveski how I had come to this career, he told me that I should be considered a "specialist" and as such he knew how I could get support, baggage transportation compensation, etc.

The list of jobs following Siberia matched my nature. I was inquisitive and was looking for a job with a pleasant environment. Jobs at several schools as a physical education teacher and coach were followed by a position as a Russian language instructor-methodologist at the Ship Repair Factory (Number 7), the head of the sports committee of the Loksa district, and sports instructor at Võsu sanatoriums. In Võsu, I played in the orchestra for about two years and then went to a similar job at Järvakandi.

I got married in 1962. My wife Mall Ojaveski (Pettai) is from Valga and a pedagogue by profession, a long-time Russian teacher (at first in Secondary School No. 14, now at Tallinn Technical Grammar School).

My teaching career had started to feel monotonous and not very lucrative, and I was lured into the job of restoring historical buildings. As an employee of the Office of Restorations, I worked on restoring many memorable buildings all over Estonia. The narrower and more fitting field for me was the work as the decor restorer and working with artificial marble. The more memorable and bigger projects were the Kadriorg Castle, the Estonian Bank building, the bathhouse of Palmse manor, and the so-called ship owner's house on Olevimägi. I also worked on the building of the Estonian Embassy in Moscow, at 5 Sobinovsky cross-street, the conference hall of the Academy of Sciences in Toompea and many churches in the Saare and Läänemaa counties.

We have raised two children: a daughter and a son. Our daughter is a dental technician, our son a musician (a guitarist). Both are married, both have two children, and both have a daughter and a son. That makes me a four-time grandfather.

As I described above, brother Toivo was not deported to Siberia. His story, however, intertwines with mine. Here it is in his own words.

Toivo Ojaveski

It was 25 March 1949, the last day of spring break. Brother Vello and I were in our room when Mother came up telling us about rumors in the village about deportations. We believed that this news did not concern us, so the next day brother Vello went to Loksa School and I went to my school in Tallinn.

What we did not know was that the deportation militia had come to my brother's school and taken both him and my mother to the train for their trip to Siberia. Apparently they were also planning to take me, but everyone feigned ignorance. When asked, they said, "He went to the city."

The deportation militia came to my living place in the city and inquired about my whereabouts. "He's in the country," was the answer. That was enough and after that, no one bothered with me. That deportation was over and I was safe. Forty years later to the day we were all rehabilitated, including myself.

With Aunt Elly's support in Muru and Aunt Meeta's support in Murumetsa I finished grades 9 and 10. I then attended Evening School IX and during the days worked at the Kivimäe grain storage. I later worked as the loan broker at the deposit bank located opposite the Baltic Railway Station. Then followed studies in Saku where I had full board. After that I worked at the agriculture department of Keila Parish as the supervisor of the department of land improvement and, after that office was closed, as the head of the land improvement group of Laitse MTJ.

Every year I was called to the military commissariat to undergo a health check to see if I would be fit for military service. I had chronic rhinitis for which I had to get my sinuses flushed out. That illness saved me. That is, until 1953. Then the paragraph was changed in the appropriate code and I was "congratulated" for being accepted into the Soviet Army. I was already 22 years old.

I gave my comb and soap box to cousin Väino and shaved my head. We were gathered at the old theater house at the beginning of Lai Street, and from there traveled as a totally drunk party to Leningrad, and from there to an unknown destination. Where we would be going was a state secret! The officers had had bad experience with *nakruts*.[14] The boys found out that we might be going to Kasakchstan and then discovered that we were to go to Siberia instead. By the time the officers sorted it out as to where they were actually supposed to be, a lot of time had passed. Because of the confusion, some more innovative guys decided to roam for months around Russia's vastness. Most rail stations had military food points, so both food and fun were to be had. We would later have three boring years staying in one place.[15]

I bought a map from a kiosk in some station and started to cross out the cities that we had been traveling through. With frequent stops we traveled for a long time – two weeks, I think – all the way along the Siberian route. Huge country! You travel days and nights, and always you see the limitless lowlands out the window.

The Sayan Mountains start in Krasnoyarsk and here we were told to get off the train, in the city where I knew my brother Vello was living. After a sauna (taps with lukewarm water) and getting into uniforms we were marched through the city at night. Here occurred the most frustrating situation of my life. We marches right past 70 Stalin Prospect, the house where I knew Vello was living. I wrote to him from the barracks and told him of my sad predicament, inviting him to meet me.

We arranged to meet at the village post office. As the appointed time arrived, I was looking around for him and studying the passengers who got off the buses. Would I recognize him? After all, four years had passed – the years of growth and development. I kept looking, but no one seemed familiar. Then my attention was caught by a man's well-polished shoes. Most people were wearing military boots or *valenki*. The man in shoes and I were looking at each other. I asked, "Is it you?" It was!

Among other things, I asked him how far away Mother was. "As the crow flies, only 400 kilometers," he replied.

From that day on we met up quite frequently, especially when I became a sergeant – then almost every weekend.

I discovered that many Estonians had been brought to Krasnoyarsk, as well as Lithuanians, Latvians, and Germans. Here I met Toomas and Jüri Kodres, Kaljo Käspre, Hilmo Seppel and others. I remember celebrating the New Year with fifty Estonian youths. We met up at some half-finished TV factory. We became very close with the family of Toomas Kodres. He spent most of his summers at Antsurahva.

My first year in service was spent in the school for sergeants. The next fall we were loaded onto the river barge *Altai* and on that we strove for many days upstream until we got to Abakan. From there our trip continued on trucks. When we had covered the agreed on distance, we asked if we were there yet. "Five more kilometers and some" was the reply. Another village. "Five more kilometers and some." And the same for the third time. That's what the understanding of distances was like.

We had arrived to harvest grain. Our destination was very close to the banks of Yenissei, on the bank of a stream that fed into it. The opposite bank was a steep rock. On two sides of the broad village road were wooden houses, most with three windows toward the road. Next

---

[14] Draftees. [Ed.]

[15] Estonian boys were subject to the draft into the Red Army but almost always were kept in their own units. The Russians did not trust the Estonians, even though they were all in the same army. The Estonian units were typically assigned to do manual labor such as field work. [Ed.]

28

to each house was a gate, and a horse gate and then the neighbor's house. The land belonging to the families was the width of the establishments to the stream behind the house. We were given one of these houses, an empty house with a single room, and in the middle of that was the famous Russian oven. We slept on the floor on trash. The army had packed us food – flour, sugar, canned food, etc. We sold that and got real food at the collective farm. Vodka was bought. I refused. Are you religious, or sick or what? That I just didn't want to drink was unheard of. In time people got used to it and there were no problems with that. Some of them joked with me. "It's OK," they laughed. "Someday we will teach you to drink vodka."

When we graduated from the school for sergeants, I received three stripes, the others got two. I was a sergeant and the others were junior sergeants. Our direct supervisor, the captain who was at the collective farm with us, must have considered me such a rare bird that it was worth noting in some way. After graduation one of the artillery battery commanders invited me to become a sergeant major. By then I had got a reputation as a non-drinker. I doubt that my secondary education was the reason. Abstinence, however, was rare. The future position necessitated financial liability and less temptation.

During grain harvest I told the captain that my mother lived close by, on the other side of the river – maybe just 100 km away. I was allowed to go and visit her. But there was no bridge on the river. The navigable river had fire buoys, and men with boats took care of them. They also ferried people across to make extra money.

I found one of the boatmen and asked to be taken across. "Let's wait for more people," he said and sure enough, more came. "Can you row, since you have no money?" he asked.

One thing we can say about the Russians: they always treated soldiers very nicely. For example, we never had to buy a bus ticket on the bus from the barracks to the city. The boatman offered to give me a free ride if I rowed.

I took to the oars. At first we traveled a long way along our bankside against the rapid current. Then we cut diagonally across the river, coming to shore at the right place, at some grain gathering point. All kinds of cars had come here. I had to get to the Horse Farm No. 42 in the Bogradsk District. A tipping truck with two oxen was going almost that way. With that I got within a half a hundred kilometers from the horse farm settlement. These were all dirt roads. When one lane became too badly rutted, the driver drove next to it. That way some roads had grown into hugely wide expanses that would only narrow at fords.

Mother was very surprised when I came in the door. Together with another Estonian woman she had bought half a house. Each had one room where they lived with their sons. Mother had a cow. She worked as an orderly at the hospital, and was sewing on her money machine, as she called it. Up until then the standard pattern for the local dressmakers was a fabric tube that had sleeve and neck holes in one end. It was tightened with a belt in the middle. Mother would sew a fitted dress and would sometimes figure out other fashion elements. That was to the Russians pure luxury.

I observed the placing of one order. A woman carrying a bundle of fabric arrived and in a rather humble manner asked Mother to sew her a dress. Mother showed her the pile of fabrics and said she did not know when she would have time. "That's not important," replied the woman. And what kind of dress do you want? "You know best."

When Mother took a piece of fabric from the pile and worked on it until it was almost ready, she sent word to the lucky person to come for fitting.

When she was back in Estonia she often complained about the Soviet government. The villagers warned her to be careful or she'd be sent back to Siberia. She would always say, "Let them; I have had as good a life there as anywhere else!"

In and around the village lived people from the displaced nation of Khakassia.[16] They were mostly horse breeders, and their droves of horses scavenged for their own food in the steppe, both in summer and in winter. The drove was kept together by the lead stallion that would bite any horse that wandered too far from the drove. The drove would be accompanied by a rider.

The most dangerous conditions occurred during strong winds. The drove would take off downwind and could dash into a deep gully. The herdsman would have to guide the mass of horses past that.

Taming the horses was amazing. The Khakassian would capture the animal to be trained with a lasso and would then jump on its back. He would have to stay there at any cost. When the horse went down to flounder, the rider would jump off, wait for the floundering to stop and then jump back on. They would race along the steppe until the animal was foaming and tired. The horse could then be considered tamed. If the horse managed to shake the rider off even once, however, the training ceased. Any horse that was able to shake a rider once would always try the same trick and thus would become untamable.

When Khruschev came to power and initiated cultivation of new lands, this state farm was turned into grain growing and the horses were butchered.

I could stay with Mother for two or three days at a time. To think how, in this massively large territory, we were brought together still amazes me.

Back at the collective farm our military unit's main task was bringing grain to the collection point, which was about 40 kilometers away. The combines gathering the grain worked night and day. Then the grain was poured on the ground about 60-80 cm deep. There they tried to dry it, tossing it with shovels from one pile to the next. It was disastrous if it happened to rain, since there was no shelter or cover. If the rain lasted for a long time the grain started to grow and was in most cases just left lying there in a pile. We saw the piles from the previous year. Rain also made our path slippery and then we just had to wait for the wind to dry the grain. If there happened to be a muddy part in the road that we could not travel on, it was also filled with grain.

At the collection point the grain was loaded on the river barges. Along the way were cliffs in some places and on those we frequently saw eagles. After my return home in 1957 a large power station with a high dam was built a bit upriver from Krasnoyarsk. This settlement was probably flooded by the reservoir.

After my unit had finished work at the collective farm and returned to base, Vello and I traveled by train to visit Mother. At Shira station we got ourselves onto a coal-filled dump truck and thus traveled along a direct winter path, often across lakes. The distance was less than 100 kilometers. Aunt Kamilla also lived in Krasnoyarsk, just on the other side of the river. She worked at the brick factory. I looked her up by her address. We had a lot to talk about.

I also tried to find Ain Paartalu, the man from our village. I only knew that he lived somewhere near the market, but there were multi-story buildings and many people. Luckily, Russians are very sociable and they know who lives in their buildings, so I asked if any

---

[16] Located in South Central Siberia, today Khakassia is a republic within the Russian Federation. [Ed.]

Estonians lived in the building. Sometimes they said yes, but it turned out to be a Lithuanian or another Baltic person. I knocked on many doors before I got to Ain. We also had a lot to talk about.

A "bad" thing was that Khruschev allowed all the deported to go back home in 1956. The majority of the deportees used that opportunity, and that brought its own traumas. When they got back they might discover that someone was already living in their home! One had to start all over again. Mother and Vello also left Siberia; I stayed there to serve for another full year. That was not a good year.

Our outfit had a four-member team of Estonians, consisting of Evgeni Kaljuste ("Prill"), Vello Kaldvee and Aleksander Minis ("Sass"), and myself. We stayed together until demobilization and even served in the same barracks. Kaljuste's mother lived in Sweden and one can only imagine how startled some parties were over their correspondence. Kaldvee and I were sergeant majors and our rooms were next to each other. We assisted each other in case of any equipment theft.

The most colorful of us was "Sass" Minis. He was from Narva and was half Russian. He took photographs of soldiers and made a business out of them. The pictures were developed at night. He spent most of the money on drinking and a lover on the other side of the barracks fence. With his lifestyle he managed to accumulate 250 days of arrest in three years. He served just a small part of it. The jail was constantly overpopulated and he simply could not fit in. He had an exceedingly happy personality. It was sheer joy to listen to his vulgar cursing in Estonian from the other end of the dreadfully morbid barracks.

It was that much more pleasant to come home at last, where at Antsurahva Mother and Vello were already waiting. Let's hope that the forced meetings with that distant location are over for good. Also, one doesn't need to be a palmist to predict a very interesting and rich future for such an empty land. How long it all will take is a different story.

Chapter 4

Malle Vesilind

It was a cold winter day when Father hurried to attach a sleigh to the horse. Mother was wrapped in warm blankets and so the fast trip to the Sakala maternity hospital in the city began. I was born on 31 January 1935.

My father, Ado (Adolf) Vesilind (1893-1975), was born in Viimsi as the youngest child. The older brothers were Eduard (1880-1947) and Otto (1883-1944). Father's parents were peasants at the Viimsi Manor. Grandfather Villem's (1861-1940) father had been a skilled sailor for the manor lord and could always stay away from the border guards' launch when carrying a load of salt or spirits on a sailboat between Estonia and Finland. That's why, when Estonians were given surnames, we were named Vesilind.[1] Grandmother's name was Liisu Tamtaal (1854-1931).

Father's early youth passed in Viimsi. After that they lived in Pirita. Grandfather occupied himself with fishing. Sprats had been very valuable in the beginning of the 1900s. Grandmother cured for their own use sprats that had been damaged during fishing. These were often without a head or tail. These cured sprats were saved for Christmas while the intact sprats were sold at the city market in Tallinn. One sprat cost half a kopek.

Living in Pirita as a small boy, Father had his own little boat. In the summer he would ferry walkers and couples on Pirita River to the Simm Island near Lükati. He was then asked to return in a couple of hours. Father said that for payment he would always hold out his hand so that the lady would be able to see what the gentleman paid. That way he would receive a silver coin, otherwise he would be given a copper coin. There was no bridge over Pirita River back then, but even without the bridge, Pirita was already a popular vacation spot.

Father was drafted into the Russian army during the First World War. He was wounded in both legs and spent half a year in a Moscow hospital. The legs were saved. Before the revolution he left Moscow on crutches. His legs healed and later he didn't use canes or crutches.

---

[1] Waterbird. [Ed.]

In 1920, together with farmer Lauba who lived by the river, Father bought a motorboat from Finland. It could transport about 50 people, and they used it to move people and goods from Pirita to Tallinn. They also hired it out for private events. Once they had a 70-member wedding party with a brass band playing on the roof. They were headed to Merivälja and the boat was so overloaded that the water was lapping over the gunwales.

I remember Father telling me how when he first went to Finland to buy the boat, he had the cash in Estonian marks but in Finland he had to pay in Russian rubles. The exchange rate at the banks would have been very bad, so he exchanged his marks behind the bank door with a Russian immigrant who was escaping from the revolution in Russia. Later in the evening he received the boat and started on his way toward Pirita alone. He was looking for the Tallinn lighthouse but soon saw the Suurupi lighthouse instead. He had gone off course by quite a bit. He had to turn left and carefully make his way to the estuary of the Pirita River.

Father's boat that carried passengers between Tallinn and Pirita. Father in the bow. To his left is his nephew Paul Vesilind.

During the summers they ran a scheduled boat line between Pirita and Tallinn. The boat line operated for thirteen years. With the new bridge over the Pirita River, a bus line was started and the boat was no longer competitive, so Father sold the boat.

From around 1921 Father ran a grocery store from rented rooms in Pirita. A large golden pretzel hung above the door.

The store was open until the Second World War when it was nationalized. Behind the store there was a little house that was called the stock room. There Father's bakers baked both black and white bread, jelly buns, and in summer also gooseberry cakes. There were also pretzels baked to order. The bread was for the people in the neighborhood and for the Kose Forest School. Flour was delivered on horse wagons belonging to the "Puhk and Sons" mill, a couple of bags of flour at a time. The horses were nice; they had thick, hairy legs.

In the store were two or three clerks in addition to Mother. Behind the store was a bakery with a baker in a white hat. Twice a year new smocks were sewn for the store clerks: for Christmas and for midsummer.

34

I remember that one day a lady with a big German shepherd came and bought ten one-day-old jelly buns, one of which was given to the dog. The store sold desiccated food, sugar, salt and candy. A ball of cheese and sausage rings were on ice in the cellar. Meat and milk were not sold. I remember a woman who would carry away the herring salting water in a small pail. The herrings were in a big barrel.

*Father's store. Mother
is second from left.*

*The bakery staff. On the far right is Mother,
and the woman in the middle is Ada. I don't
remember the names of the others.*

*My birthday.
I am in the middle with the flying hair.
Behind me are Peedu Lauba, Kristjan Kruberg,
Aino Oppi, Ilse Lauba, Kalju Soodla.*

The store had two rooms at the back – a living room and a kitchen. Lunch was made for everyone in the kitchen. I often raced with Grandfather Villem to see who could eat lunch faster. He always won. Up until the age of five I often sat at the store window, looking out.

On the Kloostri road behind the store and in front of the nunnery[2] there was a forge. The blacksmith was always grimy. I watched how a horse would agreeably place his hoof on the blacksmith's lap and how the blacksmith would then pound nails through the horseshoe into the hoof with a hammer.

In 1925 Father built a house in Pirita, eight meters wide and sixteen meters long. The builders were from Saaremaa, from Lümanda County. That's where trees were cut down in winter, cut into beams and posts, assembled, numbered, and in the spring were brought to

_____
[2] The Pirita Cloister. [Ed.]

Pirita on a ship. The ship came as close to the shore as possible, and the house beams were thrown into the water. The waves brought them on shore where men with horses were waiting. All fishermen from Viimsi and Randvere on their way home from the village market came to help. By evening, the building material was on the lot. The windows and doors were brought on shore on boats. The same Saaremaa men laid the foundation for the house. It was my home until the 1949 deportation and is my home now.

The house has seven exterior doors and three glazed verandas. In 1933 another house that had a barn, sauna, garage, and a basement on the first floor was built on the same lot. Upstairs there were eight bedrooms for summer people. By then Father had bought 21 hectares of land in Iru, at the location of the present Iru electrical station. Before the war he had no time to build anything there aside from a hay barn and a cellar. The barn had a hayrake, plow, harrow, and a hay machine that he had bought together with the neighbors. I remember how Father, a sowing tray strapped around his neck, sowed grain by hand. Only the farmer himself could perform that task. When the horse trips to Iru took place, I was often with Father. In Käru near Iru there was a mill where the grain was milled into flour and groats. A couple of times I was also taken along to look at the mill.

Our animals in Pirita included one horse, three to four cows, three to four sheep, a couple of pigs, chickens, a dog, and a cat. A farmhand assisted with the farm work, and a maid looked after the animals.

We had enough linen bedding and towels so that they could be washed twice a year – in spring and in fall. A laundry lady would assist with that job. The laundry was done in a big cauldron in the laundry kitchen that was also located in the house in the yard. One person pushed a roller from one end and the other pulled it from the other end. There was a lot of limestone on top of the roll in order to weigh it down, so it was quite hard to pull. I remember how, after slaughtering a pig, soap was made in the cauldron in the laundry kitchen. The layer of soap in the cauldron was about five to eight centimeters thick. An entire leg of pork would fit in the sauna oven for smoking. It was smoked for many days.

In all there were approximately 20 cows and 40 sheep in the Pirita farms before the Second World War. The village always hired a herdsman for the summer. In the morning the herd started moving from the farms at Kloostri road (by the bridge). Imagine what it would look like today on Merivälja Road with a 20-head herd of cows and many more sheep slowly walking down the street!

At each farm more animals were added to the herd as it went down Merivälja Road. From there it turned up Metsavahi Road and from there into the woods to graze. Metsavahi Road was as sandy as the Pirita beach. At the location of the present Pirita Grammar School there were white sand dunes. Among them grew purple thyme and bloomed small gray pasque flowers. There were also bog whortleberry shrubs.

The herdsman took turns eating at the different farms, as many days at one farm as their contribution of cows to the herd. The herdsman was clever. When it was time to go to the next farm he would first tell (I remember from his talk!) how much meat the other farms had had on the table and how semolina cream had been served for dessert. My mother then had to work hard to keep up with the others. Before Christmas the herdsman also went to all the farms where he was given potatoes, turnips and also pieces of the pig slaughtered for Christmas.

The Pirita farms had together bought a thresher and a winnower. Each fall these were set up on the Jaanson property between our house and Mart Lauri's farm. In turns, grain and peas

36

were threshed. Oh, what fun these big piles of trash were for us children, where we dug long tunnels!

Father went fishing in both the Pirita River and in the sea where he caught salmon, bream, flounder, and even eels with a bottom line. After returning from our Siberian exile, he continued to secretly fish, even though this was forbidden. Once he caught a big 15-kilogram salmon that had more than a kilogram of roe in it.

On the corner of Metsavahi and Merivälja Roads was Uncle Otto's restaurant "Brigitta."[3] I remember one lunch where we ate a bit and the waiter brought a white wash bowl with water and a towel for washing our hands.

In winter an electric saw that Father had bought together with his friend Lauba was used to cut ice on Pirita River. The slabs of ice were 1 meter long, 0.5 meter wide and 0.5 meter thick. A horse dragged those slabs of ice into a pile behind our house. When all the ice was there, the pile was covered with sawdust. In summer the ice was sold to the sausage and cheese factory. There were no refrigeration devices back then.

Pirita firefighters, 1936. In the middle is Father. On his right is Brandmann, the owner of a chocolate factory.

Before the war there was a large volunteer fire station in Pirita. Father was the team leader for the Pirita district.

My mother Frieda (née Soll) was born in Miiduranna in Viimsi as the sixth child of the family. She lived there until the age of six. Their small house caught fire when the roof was being tarred and very quickly burned to the ground. They moved to Pirita to Grandmother's brother Mart's place. Grandfather Julius Soll (1874-1946) got a job as a ranger in Kose, at the Scheel Manor. The Scheel Park reached along the Pirita River from Lükati Bridge [4] where the Scheel Manor was located to the Koch chapel. The park had nice paths, and wooden steps led from the riverbank down to the river.

Grandfather's job was to keep the entire park clean. The edges of the paths were cut straight with a shovel, the sidewalks swept clean with a broom, and the woods were cleaned of litter. There were many lilies-of-the-valley in the park. Grandfather was given a small house behind the cemetery to live in, at the location of the present sports area. On Sundays the city people would go for a walk in Maarjamäe where there are now houses. Grandfather had a stall there. On a horse he would bring lemonade from the city and sell it to the vacationers. His profits apparently were quite good.

---

[3] The Pirita Convent was built in honor of Sister Brigitta (1303 - 1373), a Swedish nun who founded the Brigitta Order. The convent was completed in 1436 and destroyed in 1575 by invading Russian troops. [Ed.]

[4] The Lükati Bridge is about a kilometer upriver from Pirita. Today there are two bridges at this location – one carries road traffic and the other is a modern wood-arch pedestrian bridge.[Ed.]

On the Pirita River by the Koch chapel there was a swimming area with wooden sides. That's where I learned to swim.

Grandmother Miina (née Elbach) (1870-1942) was a maid for the Scheels and later she was a housewife. Mother told me that as the maid's child she had a special job. On Sunday mornings when the manor lord walked from Kose to the chapel in Pirita, my mother followed him with a stool. When the lord got tired he would then have a place to sit down.

Mother started attending the Lender School in Tallinn by walking over Maarjamäe hill; the road along the sea did not exist yet. Mother lived in the house behind the cemetery until she got married.

In 1941, when the Soviet Red Army occupied Estonia, General Fedyudinsky and Sergei Kingissepp[5] chased Grandfather and half of the inhabitants of Kose out of their homes. I remember that summer day. I was outside when Grandmother and Grandfather came to our yard with their horse and carriage. They had brought a bed and a wardrobe and a few bags. The cow had been attached to the back of the carriage with a rope, and the dog Tipsi followed them. They were not allowed to go back for more things. That's how they came to live with us.

We still don't know what happened at Grandfather's house, but many people in Scheel Manor were killed during those days. Before the Russians left, they torched the manor house. When people finally had enough courage to go and see the rubble, they saw several shot horses in the yard.

With us in Pirita lived Father's son, Arnold, from his first marriage. Arnold was fourteen years older than me. In 1941 he was mobilized into the Soviet army, where he caught a cold while working in a forest and died.

When the Red Army departed Pirita in 1941, there was quite an exchange of fire between the Germans and the Russians. One of the Soviet warship commanders, as his ship was leaving the harbor, decided to destroy the standing north wall of the Pirita cloister. The ship lobbed a shell that hit the cloister, but the shell failed to explode, creating only a big hole under the middle window. That hole is there today as a reminder to the people in Pirita.

A Soviet airplane inexplicably dropped four big bombs by the woods behind our house. The windows of the house blew out, including the frames. The big bomb craters were still filled with water in 1949.

In 1942 I started attending the Kubu School (Secondary School No. 15) on Imanta Street in Tallinn. The buses went only in the morning and evening. There was a general blackout and phosphorescent flowers were pinned on coats so that people wouldn't run into each other in the street. I was able to go to school there only until January of the second grade, at which time the school was turned into a German hospital. I then went to second grade in several schools including a school on Tartu Road, one on Pärnu Road, one on Sakala Street and finally at the Pirita-Kose School. I remember two things from the Pirita-Kose school. First, in the penmanship class we had to write one line in nice handwriting for an entire hour. It was very hard to write it for that long. I also remember two boys in our class who were from the same family and who attended school on alternating days because they had only one pair of boots.

Kubu School burned down on 9 March 1944 during the air raid in Tallinn. During the air raid the sky above the city was brightly lit up – it was visible from our windows in Pirita.

---

[5] Viktor Kingisepp was the head of the Estonian Communist Party. Sergei was his son. [Ed.].

At the end of the German occupation, as the Soviet Red Army was advancing on Tallinn, Pirita Bridge (a stone bridge, built in 1936) was blown up. Red Army tanks spent several days on the damaged bridge on the city side of the river.

In 1944 I started going to Tallinn Elementary School No. 14, a small wooden house on the corner of Tatari and Allika Streets. Pirita Bridge was fixed in a couple of months. Before then one could cross the river on a boat. Korstnamäe Sass, who had a little house by the walls of the cloister, was the boatman. Father always gave me a couple of cigarettes to give to Mr. Sass for taking me across the river. From the river to the city I would go on foot. The Tallinn market was in those days between the Estonia Opera House and Pärnu Road, and on the way to school one had to go through there. If you had a few kopeks in your pocket, you could buy hard candy, which was sold by the piece. I attended that school until the 1949 deportation.

Father was labeled a *kulak*.[6] In the official documents the reasons were that there was a tenant living in the other apartment of our house and that we used seasonal help for a few days in Iru. Kulaks had to pay very high taxes, and Father was forced to quickly cut down 150 cubic meters of forest in order to pay his taxes. But it was an intentionally impossible situation. There was no way to keep up. We sold a cow, the piano, and some furniture. Father bought wood from a forester he knew near Kuusalu in order to pay previous years' government taxes. The taxes were paid, and the next day we were deported. If we only could have had that money with us...

The militia deporters came at night, at two o'clock on 25 March 1949. I was fourteen then. Mother told me to wear three dresses, one on top of each other. We didn't have a single suitcase. All our things were tossed into potato sacks. The order that we were to be deported from Estonia for life was read to us. There were four or five deporters, one with a gun and a bayonet in his hand. He stood by the door the entire time, but Mother was allowed to go to the shed with one of the deporters to fetch the sacks. We were told to bring a saw and an ax for cutting down trees, a hammer, and a water bucket to build a mud hut for ourselves. We were given one hour to pack. Father put his gloves and watch on a table by the door to pick up later but I guess the gunman liked them, because when we were leaving, they were no longer there. We were loaded onto an open truck. It was cold outside. The Pirita Lauba family was at their gate in the middle of the night and they waved to us.

We were taken to Ülemiste station and there stuffed into unlit cattle cars, where we lay on top of our bags. In the middle of the cattle car there was a door, and on both sides near the ceiling were small windows that were initially boarded up. There was an iron stove in the center. The floor of the car was one meter from the ground, with no steps. We spent the entire journey in winter coats, warm boots , and hats.

Once we crossed the border into Russia we were allowed to light the iron stove and to take the boards off the two small windows. Until then we had been in the dark. There were around fifty of us in the car. There were children aged two to six; how could they sit quietly for days? Every day we were counted to make sure no one had escaped. The door was opened briefly in Aruküla so we could go and pee in front of the car under the eyes of a gunman. That's how we squatted there, women and men together. During the journey we had to use a small hole in front of the car door.

---

[6] Originally a *kulak* was a successful farmer, but in later years any small businessman who profited from his work was called a *kulak*. Stalin labeled *kulaks* as a class and vowed to eliminate them by murder or deportation. [Ed.]

Tapa was the next stop, and there we were allowed to bring drinking water in buckets into the car. On the third day we were given about half a liter of soup and a piece of bread. We luckily had homemade bread, groats, meat, and flour with us. That's how we traveled for fourteen days, in winter coats, lying on top of our bags.

The first off-loading was on 7 April in Atchinsk. There ten cars, including ours, were unhooked from the train. We were put on trucks, and the journey continued along icy and snowy fields for two days. At our first stop a sauna had been prepared for us and our clothes were put in a lice-killing chamber. On the second day the journey continued when bags, children, and old people were loaded on sleighs, while the others had to follow the sleighs on foot and push the sleighs when required to do so. The winter roads were breaking down.

Late in the evening we reached Birilyussky. We had covered 25 kilometers in a day. In the early morning of 9 April we continued on with the horses along Tsulym River, a tributary to the Ob River. By evening we reached a collective farm by the name of Polevoy. There we were housed in the club room.

The "slave market" took place the next day. Father bragged about his skills and said that he was a *krupnyi spetsialist po motoram,*[7] and so our family was ordered to work at the Machine-Tractor Station. Everyone had to sign a document acknowledging that they knew that they had been deported to Siberia for life and that they would be shot if they tried to escape. Two years later, as a member of a *kulak* family, I also signed such a document when I turned sixteen.

Workers at the Motor-Tractor Station. Second row from the right, Olvi, me, and Father. Mother is in front right, seated.

Twenty-two people were put to work at the Machine-Tractor Station. For a couple of weeks all 22 of us were also housed in a single room. The room was big enough that all of us could sleep on the floor. It was the seventeenth day after the journey had started, and for the first time we could look for clean underwear in our bags and be able to wash ourselves. We were covered with lice.

From then on we were spread out in the house. Nine of us stayed in the same apartment. There was a small 3x3 meter kitchen with a Russian oven, small 2x3 meter room where two men slept, and a room the length of which housed the seven of us to sleep side by side on the floor: me, Father, Mother,

---

[7] Great specialist in engines. [Ed.]

Mrs. Murusalu with her five-year-old son and Mr. and Mrs. Mandri. The width of the room was a bit greater than our height.

The other deportees were put to work at the collective farm. Mother and I went to buy salt in the village store, but they didn't have it there, so we had to trade with a local collective farmer. For half a glass of salt Mother had to trade a lace curtain.

On midsummer night the Estonians built a large fire outside the village and there was a lot singing. The next day a new order came for us to pack up again. We were given horses to carry our bags, but we had to walk on foot to the river where an open barge was waiting for us.

Three days of traveling, on top of our bags again, along the Tsulym River to the city of Atchinsk. At day's end we were allowed to go on shore, to a deserted place where there was nowhere to escape. There were many mosquitoes.

The river was complex and the crew was drunk, so Father took the wheel and steered the barge for two days. The crew later gave him a plateful of food which he brought to us. We were housed in a big gymnasium. A few days later we started the journey south by train, to Khakassia.

We traveled for a day and night, again sitting on top of our bags. It was summer and warm. At the Kopyiovo railway station we were taken off the train. It was 7 July. For the next 100 kilometers we had to travel by open truck. We began to see tree-covered mountains. We traveled through Sarala, the district center of Saralinsk and Gidra – there was a big power station there – to Glavstan village. Here there was another slave market. We were split between several villages. Six kilometers away was a gold mine. We settled in at our new home, Glavstan.

Sarala River ran by the village but the water was gray and toxic because it had been used and discharged by the gold mining operation. The river banks glittered in gold. Our village was quite large and spread in three directions from the center, with houses alongside the road. The cars could drive as far as to our village in winter, but from there the lumber to support the mine had to be hauled by horses along the frozen river.

The small houses of the locals consisted of a loosely boarded front room, kitchen and another room that had a couple of beds. In the kitchen were a table and a bed. To the end of the bed a calf would be tied in winter. Under the table behind a wire mesh were chickens. In the front room there was room for a cow. Actually there were only a few cows in our village, and in summer they did not give more than ten liters of milk a day.

The pigs had collars put around their necks to keep them out of the vegetable garden. The cows grazed in a mountain pasture in summer. The mistress would in the evening go on a hill and call, "tsyilia, tsyilia" and a cow would call back from far away in the mountains and come home. Outside the village was a big hospital consisting of several buildings. They even had an X-ray machine, drugstore, and dentist. Minor operations were also performed there. Some Russian girls, after they finished grade 7, had one of their front teeth pulled and replaced with a gold tooth.

There was a seven-grade school in the village, a store, a club house, a post office and a common sauna. The sauna, which could hold at least ten people, had a steam room, washing room with benches and a shower. It was heated every week and it was free. Movies were shown every week at the club house.

The people in our village had all been deported in 1930, and most of their husbands had been taken away. There were Volga Germans, Crimean Tatars, Moldovans, Carpathians, and men from the Vlassov army.[8]

At first we lived with a local. Later we had a room in a twin house, only about 3x3 meters but at least it was private. Two wooden cots for sleeping, a stove with a hot wall, a small table and two stools fit in the room. We could also plant potatoes by the house. All the houses in our village had low doors; you had to bend down to enter so as not to hit your head. Toilets were not known in the village.

Father got a job at the garage. Mother first worked at the sewing workshop. On the night of the deportation Mother had unscrewed her Singer sewing machine from its base and taken it with her. At first Mother would sew as Father would crank the wheel with his finger, but later Mother's brother had managed to buy a hand crank from the flea market.

Father and Mother at Glavstan Village, 1952.

At home Mother could only hem bed sheets, but now she started sewing *kalifeks*[9] for men, which were in fashion, and *fufaikas*[10] and multicolored quilts (she hand-stitched the patterns which were only in the corners; the center just had the squares). She later started sewing dresses for the wives of the mine management. She was given magazines with pictures to follow as examples. We had no copy paper, so the pattern was drawn on a newspaper and that was stitched onto the dress. As payment for the pants that she sewed for the store keeper's husband, Mother got a new pair of valenki for me each winter.

The neighboring village, Verkas, initially had open gold mine *artels*.[11] There was some kind of a chute into the ground and from there enriched soil was pulled out in buckets and washed in troughs. The workers were not paid in money but in coupons. The store had better things for sale for coupons so that we had to exchange money to get the coupons. Canned whale was cheaper in coupons, for example. Those artels were soon closed down.

Using yokes, we brought water from a brook.

---

[8] General Andrei Vlassov was a Russian general during the Second World War, leading an army of White Russians who deserted en masse and fought with the Germans against the Red Army. After the war he was returned to the USSR and hung. Most of his men were machine gunned as they got off the trains.[Ed.]
[9] Heavy German military field pants. [Ed.]
[10] Heavy Russian military coats. [Ed.]
[11] An *artel* is a peasants' cooperative. [Ed.]

I had outgrown my coat so Mother made me a beautiful black satin *fufaika* with a gray rabbit fur collar that she took from her own old winter coat.

I went again to grade 7, which I had already finished, and repeated exams in Russian and history. For half a year I didn't really understand anything. I also didn't have a dictionary. In gym class I was told to put a skirt on top of the track pants because it was not proper to wear pants. My first dictation was more red than blue, the ending of some words written together with the beginning of the next, as I could not understand what the words were. In history I was asked the dates for the Russian emperors and kings and wars. I did not know any of this. At first there were no notebooks and we wrote on printed booklets.

I attended secondary school six kilometers away at the Priskovo gold mining village and lived at the dorm, four to five girls in a room. I went home every week. We cooked for ourselves. Bedding and blankets were given by the school.

The first evening at the dorm as I was getting ready for bed I put on my nightgown. The other girls had never seen such a thing and they made fun of me. Later I did not put on a nightgown but slept in my underwear like the rest of them.

The wooden cedar floors had to be cleaned each week by scraping them with a knife.

The typical meal was potatoes fried in oil, half a bucket a week, and bread that I had brought from home in a backpack. I didn't buy milk and we had no meat or carrots. Russians don't eat turnips, nor do they eat potato skins.

The first snow appeared on the peaks of the mountains at the end of August and did not melt until the end of May. In winter there were frequent snowstorms. From between the mountains the wind was always blowing in one direction, against us as we were walking to school. On the river was the sleigh path. When a gust of wind came, you had to turn your back to the wind, find something to support yourself, such as an uneven spot on the road or a pile of frozen horse manure. Otherwise the wind would lift you up and carry you for several meters until you hit some obstacle. You were lucky if you stayed on your feet. In such a storm you frequently had to thaw out your eyelashes. The rest of the face was covered with a scarf. In the wind, arms would freeze first. It felt like being pierced by needles. When the wind became very strong, the sauna pipe sounded several times (it was used as a siren), as a warning not to go to school.

The schoolhouse was relatively big, a hall in the middle and on three sides probably seven classrooms. The hall even had a piano. A stream ran behind the school, and on the bank of that was the school outhouse – a wooden shed with spaced boards and a hole in the floor. The wind blew through, the air was clean and everything went into the stream. The houses were built so that wind would blow the snow away from the door. The windows of the school were towards the wind so that the snow drifted up to the gutters while the door was clear of snow.

The mountains were covered in cedar forest. I ate many cedar nuts. It was dangerous to go to the forest because of the bears. When a bear wandered into the village we ate bear meat!

At Priskovo School Estonians Olvi Särgava (Kuusik), Erich Talmar, Valdeko Ratassepp, and Irene Lepikson (Mahlak) studied with me. The elementary grades had more Estonians. In hindsight we had very good and smart teachers, especially in math. In the last grade I took part in a mathematics Olympiad organized by Tomsk University and received a certificate.

I went to the center in Gidro, 25 kilometers away, for the last grade in secondary school and lived at the dorm. There were seven of us in the room. It was full of bedbugs. Putting the bed legs in bowls of water did not help. The bugs jumped on you from the ceiling at night.

I went home from there once a month, usually riding on a truck. Once I decided to walk. It was a nice sunny and cold winter day and I figured 25 kilometers would be nothing. But it was and I was very tired after that trip. In hindsight, I realize a bear could have appeared from behind a tree. I did not meet a single soul on the journey, nor did anyone pass me. On this 25 kilometer stretch there was just one small village with a few houses.

At Gidro were fellow Estonian students Rita and Tiia Aire, Helve Seppik, Aarne Välja, and Vladimir Borsakovski. There were others of our age but they didn't study. We often spent time together in the evenings.

The mountainsides were very beautiful in the spring, full of single red peonies, tall blue bellflowers, big white daisies and dark yellow globeflowers.

In July of 1954 Olvi and I traveled to Krasnoyarsk to start studies at the Siberian Institute of Forest Technology. When we got off the train there was a crowd in front of the station building. There we were, two country bumpkins, suitcases in hand and no clue as to where to go. So I straddled the two suitcases while Olvi went to find out where the bus stop was located. Men in tattoos with bare upper bodies and wide pants started walking around me. It was the time when after the death of Stalin the prisoners in the big prison camps at the mouth of the Yenissei had been granted amnesty and were set free. They came down along Yenissei on ships and were waiting at the station to continue their journey. That was my first impression of Krasnoyarsk. Luckily they didn't bother me.

Olvi and I were accepted at the institute, me in the forest technology department, Olvi to the mechanics department. The competition was severe, with many more people applying than would be accepted. Luckily this university accepted students without passports, which all the other universities required. The only documents we had were pieces of paper that said that we were *spetspereselenka* – deported. Each month we had to go to the local commandant to give a signature to prove that we had not escaped. At the commandant's, after presenting our student identification, we were given a new paper that said we could live only in the territory of the city of Krasnoyarsk. I had to apply for a permit to visit Mother and Father.

The more eager deportees had gathered in Krasnoyarsk to get out of the collective farms and mines. There were more than twenty of us Estonians in the universities and technical schools of Krasnoyarsk. There were also many Latvians and Lithuanians. We associated with each other a lot. We all lived with the help of scholarships.

During the first summer we spent almost two months helping harvest grain at a collective farm, walking with sticks in front of the combine and lifting the fallen grain, then cleaning it with a winnowing machine.

I began to understand the life of a Russian collective farmer. The potato field was so large that you couldn't see the end of it. It was a plain field of black soil – no furrows where the potatoes should have been planted. Perhaps they were in square clusters? We were given wooden sticks, and with these we had to find the potatoes. By the evening we had a couple of wagons full of potatoes.

Olvi and I decided we were lucky that our family had ended up at a mining village and not on a collective farm. Even the two of us, young able-bodied people, could not fill our daily quota and would have ended up owing the collective farm.

Our food that summer consisted of two bowls of cabbage in boiling water a day and a few slices of bread. We slept on the floor of the club house in the same clothes that we worked in.

44

Krasnoyarsk was a big city on the banks of the Yenissei River. The forest technology institute was in a large building on the main street, Stalin Prospect. We were young, and the two years I spent there were very enjoyable. In the winter, in February, the temperature dropped to – 36°C, and we were waiting for the thermometer to rise to – 25 so we could get warm. At those temperatures your cheekbones become covered in white blotches from the cold.

The first year I rented a room together with Olvi at a Russian woman's apartment. She had three small rooms and a kitchen. She rented one room to us, about 2x3 meters. We slept in the same bed, which had wood boards for a bottom and no mattress. We have tried to remember what we ate there, but we can't. In any case it wasn't milk, meat, butter or potatoes.

We did not cook anything aside from boiling water for tea. The cafeteria at the university had soups with small pieces of meat, as well as soups without meat. The meatless soups were half the price of the meat soups. So we ate the meatless soups, along with some slices of bread and some porridge.

During the second year, together with Ipe (Kobin) Vernik we rented a room with a private entrance through the yard. The room had a stove with a hot wall and two wooden cots. We bought a cubic meter of firewood for the winter. That was all we could afford. We would go to the station to look for dropped coal and scavenged behind the store to gather pieces of broken boxes. An electrician had lived in our room and he had connected the socket in our wall to the electric post in the street, behind our window. Into that socket we connected a small electric stove, which was our only source of heat. We had it on night and day. Only the small light bulb in the ceiling went through the electric meter.

Our welcome at the Baltic Railway Station, 6 August 1956.

The cockroaches also loved the heat. When we came home from school and moved the stove to prevent the floor from catching fire, the cockroaches ran out like rays of the sun. We even had a reproductor[12] on the wall of our room, which woke us up with the USSR anthem in the morning. A couple of times Georg Ots'[13] singing would sound from it, too.

The two years in Krasnoyarsk, 1954-1956, were very nice years of my youth, despite the fact that my clothes were very poor (re-done from Mother's old clothes) and our accommodations were sparse. The locals, of course, weren't any better off.

In the spring of 1956 came

---

[12] Speaker tuned to a single channel [Ed.].
[13] Georg Ots (1920 – 1975) was a famous Estonian operatic singer [Ed.].

exemption from the exiles' life sentences. I took my last exams, went to Mother and Father's and from there we traveled together to Tallinn. Before departure Mother collected all our bedding, towels, underwear and other clothing, almost all of which was bought sixteen years earlier before the war. She built a big fire behind the house and burned everything. The old pot and pan that we had with us also went into the fire, along with the plates that had long since been broken. We brought Mother's sewing machine back with us, however.

We waited for an entire day and night for the tickets at the Atchinsk railway station. We were taken to Siberia for free, but had to pay for the return journey. We could have, of course, voluntarily stayed there.

The journey to Moscow took three days and nights, and from there to Tallinn another day and night. Siberia had not gotten the best of us. We came back alive and well. Many relatives and acquaintances met us at Baltic Station.

University student.

We found temporary residence at Mother's relative's place. A few months later we got a place to live in one of the outbuildings on Metsavahi tee in Pirita. After that we found a small 15 square meter room in Mähe where my parents lived until their deaths.

By accident I had received a passport in Krasnoyarsk that didn't have the residence restriction stamp in it. I took my papers to the Tallinn Polytechnic Institute and I was accepted to the second year, to the engineering department.

Two years later I transferred to the evening division and graduated from the institute in 1961 as an industrial and civil engineer. Today, the degree is equivalent to the master's degree.

While I was a student I had already been working at the Estonian Industrial Project at the drafting table. In 1965 I started working as an engineer-constructor at "Tsentrosojuzprojekt" and worked there until my retirement. I participated in designing industrial buildings, trade buildings and bread factories. We also designed templates of those for the entire Soviet Union, including the ones in permafrost zones. After I retired from engineering work I worked for three years as the receptionist at Õismäe clinic.

In 1965 I got a co-op apartment in Mustamäe. In 1977 my son Andres was born. At the age of 30 Andres was awarded a doctorate degree in economics from the University of Tartu. He has three daughters and a son.

In 1994 I was given back Father's house in Pirita and the farm in Iru. There was a power station built in Iru, so of the 21 hectares I got back only nine. It's clear land without a

Restored Pirita house on Metsavahi Street.

46

single tree but in parts there are high voltage lines and towers. The land was divided into plots and I sold some and gifted some to Andres.

Our old house on Metsavahi was in terrible shape. Fifty years of neglect is a long time. The wood shingle roof had been destroyed in the war and had been replaced by slate. Water and sewer had been brought into half of the house while half of it was still on a septic tank. The veranda windows had been boarded shut.

In the main house lived decent people, but in the small house in the yard lived drunks. In time I found new places for all of them, two to an old age home, two to a nursing home, and some received new apartments from the state.

Andres got married, needed a place and immediately started renovations. The exterior of the house was restored to its former look. Inside, modern renovations were made. The supporting structures we did not dare touch. Some of the veranda lace windows were preserved and we restored all the veranda windows based on their patterns. I moved to Pirita in 2008.

As I look back at what I have written, the story of my life has become a description of life in Pirita, my ancestors and the years of my youth in Siberia. I want my grandchildren to know what life was like in Pirita in the old days and then what life was like in Siberia. I want them to know that if there is enough will, one can survive and even prosper under any circumstances.

Chapter 5

Rein Saluvere

In 1954 my father was working in the Forestry Center of Tachtyp in Khakassia at the upper course of the Abakan River. In early spring of 1957 he announced that together with his wife Linda and two half-brothers Lembit and Jaan they had decided to go back to Estonia. He recommended I go, too. Life in Estonia was supposedly much more sensible.

But in considering the return to Estonia I had to think of all that I would be leaving.

During the school year 1948/49 I had been attending Secondary School No. 1 in Võru. The March deportation occurred during the spring break. When we returned to school after the break, a mood like a post-funeral pall hung over the class. The same occurred all over Estonia. Many seats in my class remained empty. Our Russian teacher had also been taken away. He had apparently been a member of the White Army.[1]

Deportation was not enough for the Soviets. The hysterics about class struggle, bourgeois nationalism, firings, and arrests had started. Father, who had worked as the chief engineer at the Rakvere Forestry Center, was fired.

In March of 1951 I had been seeing Dr. Põkk at the Tartu surgical clinic because in the summer of 1949 I had been diagnosed with bone tuberculosis in my right foot. The foot was put in a cast and I was put on crutches.

During one check-up at the clinic in Tartu a security officer and a female interpreter met me at the hospital procedures room. They took me to a gray house in Tartu where for the first three days I sat on a stool without being allowed to sleep. Interrogations took place at night. On the fourth night, after our home in Rakvere had been searched, I was sent upstairs where I could lie down on a table covered with a red cloth. The next day I was on the train to Rakvere.

In Rakvere I learned that in addition to the search, a provocateur[2] had also been to our place, a very polite young man who had wanted to meet me. The meeting luckily did not happen, and all he could do was inform his superiors that I was at the clinic in Tartu.

---

[1] The Russian civil war was fought between the White Army, a loosely allied group opposed to the Bolsheviks, and the Bolshevik Red Army. After the war, once the Bolsheviks were in power, former members of the White Army were systematically eliminated. [Ed.]

[2] A provocateur is a person who tries, through friendly discussion, to get incriminating evidence against someone. [Ed.]

Cousin Maie was also visited by a provocateur. She was fooled by him and as a result spent many years in a prison camp. The issue was that cousin Tõnis, who had spent summers with us, apparently had been a member of the Tartu University students' organization *Sinimustvalge* ("Blueblackwhite.")[3] On the night before the October holiday they had blown up a bronze statue of a soldier in Raadi and done possibly something else. Neither Maie nor I were even aware of the organization, but the security officers did not believe us.

A Moscow colleague of Father had suggested to him, "Perhaps for a while you should work at another region in the Soviet Union." With my arrest, this advice carried more weight. Father first went alone and, once he had found a job, wrote to tell us to come join him. This is how his wife Linda and I wiped the dust of Estonia from our boots. My sister and brother stayed in Estonia.

At the end of April, when we arrived at the forestry settlement of Tupik in the Shira District of Khakassia, our fears subsided. A year later we already had a cow, chickens and we had even slaughtered our first pig. We were doing well enough to consider sending parcels to Estonia. Our parcels would have been much better than the parcels that came from Estonia during the years 1949-1951.

In 1955 I finished Shira middle school. During my days there I had been living with the widow of Estonia's former President[4] Jaam Teemant, Alide-Emilie Teemant. Although her health was not good she still managed to return to Estonia after being allowed to do so. She died in 1961 and is buried in Tallinn.

After graduation I traveled to Krasnoyarsk where I entered the program in agricultural mechanics.[5]

We had a reasonable life and there was no rush to return to Estonia. I consider my six years in Krasnoyarsk successful. The bone tuberculosis had settled down; I had spent two years in a secondary school and two years in the mechanization department of the agricultural institute.

I had good memories of Estonia, but I also began to realize that nature had not distributed its bounties evenly. Even in the one-sixth of the globe where we at least theoretically could freely move around, there were places where Damskie Palchiki tomatoes[6] ripened and many other exotic things could be found.

That's how I started to weigh returning to Estonia, or rather leaving Krasnoyarsk. Why could I not continue my studies in a more exotic location than Estonia? Many universities in the Soviet Union had similar departments with presumably matching curricula (agricultural mechanization) at least for the first two years, which by then I had finished. I studied the brochures and decided to go to Stavropol. I was cautious about Caucasus, and Central Asia also didn't appeal to me, but I still wished for shorter winters, longer summers and falls, and a location with grapes in the neighborhood.

I was also hesitant to leave Krasnoyarsk because I did not want to leave my good friend Peet Treikelder with whom we had found a small apartment. But at last the issue was decided and the rail ticket bought.

---

[3] The colors of the national flag. [Ed.]
[4] He was actually not called "president" but *riigivanem*, or "national leader". [Ed.]
[5] Today we would call this field "agricultural engineering". [Ed.]
[6] A small, luscious, plum tomato. [Ed.]

50

Yenissei River in Krasnoyarsk.

Shira district of Khakassia, south of Krasnoyarsk.

Allan   Juta   Rein   Beate   Kaljo

Estonian students at Krasnoyarsk.

Rail tickets in the Soviet Union remained valid for much longer than the anticipated journey. For example, the trip from Krasnoyarsk to Tallinn was supposed to be about five days, but the ticket was valid for 14 days. During that time one could make stops on the chosen route and then continue the journey on the next train. It was much cheaper to travel on one long-distance ticket than to buy several tickets to cover the same distance. That's how the ticket from Krasnoyarsk to Sochi was bought (through Moscow). I wanted to visit Shira and see my secondary school desk mate Nikolay Šartse, stop in Stavropol, take the ship across the Black Sea to Odessa and from there ride the train from Odessa to Leningrad to Estonia. One has to think big.

I arrived in Moscow on the Krasnoyarsk-Sochi ticket when the World Youth Festival was taking place (1957). The Šartse family was at the time living in the Moscow suburbs and had to take the electric train to Moscow. The Šartses were Russian emigrants who had in 1954 returned to Russia from China. Nikolay's father had in his day been an officer in the Koltchak army[7] and probably didn't have a proper job in China. Nikolay's mother had worked at an English ship company in China and was now specializing in translating Russian literature into English. Before attending Shira secondary school Nikolay had studied in the local English college in China. By the time of my visit to Moscow, he had finished two years at the law department of the Moscow State University. The Šartses' second home language was English and Nikolay had got a job as an interpreter at the festival. I took part in some of the festival events with him. I remember the performance of Arkadi Raikin[8] at the assembly hall.

Walking on Red Square, we noticed a group of Chinese women. They asked Nikolay if he could speak Chinese, and the meeting ended with a group photo. Later on I asked Nikolay about his Chinese language skills. He admitted that at the war commissariat he had denied his knowledge of Chinese.

Another moment I remember of that grand event in Moscow is how interested the local girls were in Negroes.

I tried unsuccessfully to photograph the festival's closing fireworks on the bank of the Moscow River.

The next morning I was on the train heading south. Many people in the Soviet Union wanted to go south in the summertime. After a day and night on the train I climbed off at Armavir. Already during that early morning the heat was intense.

At the Stavropol Institute, the one I had picked out of the brochure, there was great confusion in the enrollment of students. At the same time it was hard to find the official who would be interested in my offer and be empowered to make a decision. I don't recall what the title of the man was who was listening to me while doing other things, but he quickly gave a negative response. I sauntered away from the institute and finally managed to find a bed at the so-called farmers' homes near the market.

The heat became the main problem with the trip south. I tried to relieve the situation by consuming lots of water from the sparkling water machines. I started sweating a lot and the thirst grew. I was quite done. Climate sickness. It seemed I also developed a fever.

---

[7] Admiral Koltchak was a controversial figure during the Russian civil war. A former officer in the army that Koltchak led would find some difficulty living in Bolshevik Russia. [Ed.]
[8] Arkady Isaakovich Raikin was a Soviet stand-up comedian. [Ed.]

The horrible experience in that land convinced me that I should go back to Estonia. I thought of going to either Tallinn or Tartu. My sister was studying in Tartu and we also had relatives there. The next trip was therefore to Tartu.

In Tartu there were no problems with filling out the documents at the Estonian Agricultural Academy, but I needed a fountain pen for the application. Many important-looking people were in the hallways and the vestibule, but I needed to find a Soviet student whom I could ask to borrow a fountain pen without being embarrassed.

Finally the application was written. For the next three years I was a student at the mechanization department of the Estonian Agricultural Academy.

When I went to collect my passport at the Tartu registration office, I was told to go and talk to the supervisor. An older rough-voiced woman was sitting in the office. She was interested in why I had lived in Krasnoyarsk. I explained that I was a normal Soviet citizen and that I could live wherever I wanted to in this great country. This did not satisfy her. She promised to investigate.

Even though Khrushchev had liberalized everyday life, there was still the need to "investigate."

Chapter 6

Toomas Kodres

I was born in Tallinn in 1935 to Mother Elvi Kodres and Father Jüri Kodres. My father was deported to Russia on 14 June 1941 and was shot to death on 14 September 1942 in the city of Solikamsk in the Perm district of the Russian SSR.

I began my schooling in Tallinn, at the Tallinn Secondary School No. 21 on Raua Street.

In 1949 my entire family was deported to Siberia (Krasnoyarsk territory, district of Nazarov, Krasnopolyanski Myaso-Molotchnoi collective farm.) I was accompanied by my brother Jüri Kodres, Mother Elvi Kodres, Grandmother Minna Lentsius, and Aunt Amanda Lentsius. There was no documentation of the charges; we were never told what crime we had committed.

In Siberia we were housed in a hut – in a single room together with another three-member family. In that one small room lived eight people. We had a small stove for heating. I spent most of my time doing field work plus gathering firewood in the forest. The collective farm had no school and there were no options or time for studying. In a couple of years we found it possible to move to the village of Nazarov. There my job was to make furniture in the wood shop, and in the evening I could attend school. I completed the courses in the evening school and found it possible to attend the Physical Education Technical School at Krasnoyarsk.

With Harri at the Krasnoyarsk Railroad Workers Club.

I was freed in the fall of 1957 and returned to Estonia, but I had no place to live and could not register an address. Regardless of my diploma, I could not get work. Six months passed like that. I spent nights wherever I happened to be and spent the days looking for work. Finally a militia officer helped me to register a temporary place of residence at a fictitious address. With that I was able to get a temporary job.

With fellow Estonian students
Vello and Õilme.

I got a sports job at the Marat knit garment factory, and from there I was promoted to lead the sports team of the construction and renovation division of the same company. I was then invited to direct the sport work department of the Estonian Railroad, and from there I went to work as a physical education teacher at Tallinn Secondary School No. 13.

I continued my studies in physical education at the Tallinn Pedagogical Institute and branched out to studies in manual training. Following graduation, I became a teacher at the Tallinn Tuberculosis Treatment Center, and then finally I was hired by the Tallinn Secondary School No. 44, where I worked for 29 years.

After that I gave up teaching and went into business for myself. My first company, AS T. Kodres, was in the field of food retail. My second company, OÜ TOKO Group, was in the wholesale business of bathroom décor and photography.

I have divested my interest in the companies and am now retired, spending my time traveling and with my three grandchildren.

Estonian students' party along the shores of the Katša River.

Chapter 7

Olvi Kuusik

I was born in the cold midwinter, 21 February 1936, in the Republic of Estonia, the 18th anniversary of the Declaration of Independence, in what is now Türi County, Laupa Village Lehtmetsa farm. My father was from the same area and was my grandfather's second son. My grandfather had been drafted into the Estonian military during the War of Independence (1918 – 1920). He had been just 22 years old when he returned from the war. He had served with distinction and was awarded the Cross of Liberty and was also granted land by the state (with a redemption clause),[1] land that used to belong to Laupa manor.

I had three older brothers who all attended the Laupa Manor School.[2] When my brothers were born they had been given the surname Peterson. This was a very old family name that can be traced back to the seventeenth century in the records of the Vändra church. Apparently there had been a Peter, of unknown nationality, who had invaded the area and decided to stay, hence the family name of Peterson. My grandmother also was related to the Petersons.

In 1935 the extended family, led by Ernst Peterson, who was an educator, writer, and Member of Parliament, decided to Estonianize the family name. They chose the name Särgava, which was a modification of the farm name, Särghaua. I was the first child born Särgava.

The neighboring farm to Särghaua is the Kurgia farm. This was, during the time of Estonia's independence, a very prosperous farm that worked at a high agritechnical level. My Aunt Kati, who was my father's sister, was the last mistress of the farm. She was also deported in 1949 to Siberia, along with my Aunt Leena, who had owned shares at the Põltsamaa dairy farm and was the dairy manager at the farm. Both of my father's sisters were my godmothers and undertook seriously their obligations to me. If things had worked out differently, I might have become Aunt Leena's heir and a dairy manager! Aunt Kati died during the deportation somewhere near Omstk, but Aunt Leena reached her destination at Baikal-Ankara.

My uncle, Aunt Leena's husband, when informed that Aunt Leena had been deported, hid himself and their children to avoid being similarly arrested. Later, however, he volunteered

---

[1] Redemption in legal terminology refers to a seller's right to repurchase something sold by returning the purchase price to the buyer.[Ed.]
[2] In 2008, Laupa Manor School was voted the most beautiful school in Estonia.

to go to Siberia to help with the hard work. Both of my aunts were over 60 years old when they were taken to Siberia. My uncle, who was probably closer to 70 years old, worked for seven years in forestry in Siberia. This location today is a research base for geologists of the Institute of Geology.

The family Peterson-Särgava, 1938.

With brothers Feliks and Paul, 1949, in Tallinn.

My family has a confusing genealogy. My grandfather Jaan was also born on this farm in 1843 and died before I was born. My paternal grandmother's ancestors also came from the same farm. Mother's parents lived in the same area while Grandfather was a farmhand of the Särevere manor. All of my grandmothers and great grandmothers were manor maids. With all of this farm background in our family, it is curious that none of the children in my generation became rural people.

The family's farm life came to an end when my father, who had been farming for 15 years, was forced to sell his cattle to cover a loan his brother-in-law had made and which he had co-signed. My father at the time was a parish council member but this did not help.

By this time my father had also developed a serious heart problem and was unable to continue his work on the farm, so the farm was rented out. Our family moved first to Türi, later to the town of Valga, where Father got a government job at the rail traffic administration, as a steward on the Viljandi route. But this did not last for long. My mother was working as a helper during potato harvesting season in a nearby farm and caught a cold, got sick with pleurisy and was taken to Tartu Clinic. She remained there for four months. She was so sick that she was even unaware of the situation at home or that her husband had suddenly died before Christmas of 1938. He was buried in the Türi central cemetery.[3]

With my father dead and my mother unable to care for me, the paternal sisters determined our fate. My two older brothers were sent to Põltsamaa to learn metal and wood processing, and I was sent to Tallinn to complete my primary education under the supervision of Aunt Elsa. Aunt Elsa, who would become the most important person in my life, had a certificate from the Kehtna Home Economics School and worked as a weaver for "Tallinn Kodukasitöö"[4] (currently ARS). She had a home workshop and a rented apartment. The plan had been, when I was born, to name me after Aunt Elsa, but since this name was not of Estonian origin and a new Estonian law forbade giving children non-Estonian names, I was named Olvi, a name that my father had apparently found on the back of a calendar.

At the age of three I was baptized at the Türi church and added to their list of parishioners.[5] My sickly mother, who after my father's death had lost health insurance and was thus released from the hospital, also came. She eventually recovered and lived for another 52 years.

She eventually got a survivor's pension and a government job as the car cleaner at the Tallinn Tram Car Depot. With Mother we moved in with Aunt Elsa in Pelgulinn. Later Mother worked as a tailor at the railway studio, a job for which she had the appropriate training.

I think that if Father had lived we would have been deported to Siberia with the 1941 deportees, but our family had dispersed and was therefore difficult to track. My youngest brother graduated from the Lai Street Primary School No. 18 and went on to the railway school, while my older brothers went to the Tallinn Industrial Technical School (TTT). In 1943 Aunt Elsa took me to the Lai Street Primary School (Ratassepa School), which after the Soviet air raid of 9 March 1944 was turned into a hospital. After the raid my desk mate disappeared. Her house in Kalamaja had been destroyed.

When the Germans came, they gave us back our farm that the Russians had "given" to the renters. My mother moved to the farm, and during the German occupation she paid off all the farm debts. As fate would have it, the farm became a battleground between the Germans and the Soviet Red Army. We lived through numerous battles as the farm changed hands between the Germans and the Russians. Several times we, along with the tenant family and the cattle, hid in the woods waiting for the battle to end.

When the front passed by, the farm buildings remained, but we were robbed of all potential supporting or construction material, which had been carried away to the battle trenches. Residential building construction remained unfinished after Father's death, and building materials were in short supply.

---

[3] During the Soviet time this cemetery became a park.
[4] Home handcrafts. [Ed.]
[5] Türi, Estonia's Spring Capital, is a beautiful city. It's the home of the Suisa-Päisa choir. Türi is supposed to have the happiest cows in Estonia!

Once when we were hiding in the woods I came face to face with a German officer on horseback who said to me, "*Auf Wiedersehen!*" He then saluted me and gave me a chocolate bar – my first war booty. This time the Russians had been forced to retreat, but the battles left behind two German graves near the house by the roadside.

We went back to Tallinn as soon as possible. My youngest brother Paul, who was sixteen years old at the time, had been spending the summer working as a farmhand at a distant relative's farm. He did not make it back to Tallinn in time before the Russians retook the capital.

In 1943 my oldest brother Felix (1924) was mobilized by the Germans and was sent to basic training. He was lucky because he became a cartographer at the German headquarters in Narva. The middle brother Otto (1925) would also have been drafted by the Germans except that my mother decided to hide him. He attempted to escape by boat to Finland, as the "Finnish Boys"[6] were doing at the time. However, the ice conditions did not allow the boat to dock in Helsinki harbor and he had to come back to Estonia, where he voluntarily surrendered to the German border guards. He was imprisoned in the Patarei Prison under a false name. He had in his pocket the German passport of a good family friend, an Estonian military officer who had fallen in the Czech Republic. But the name had been included in the list of fallen officers and Felix was found out. By that time Tallinn was under siege by the Soviet Red Army and the prisons were emptied.[7] The greatest irony was that the warden at the prison during the German occupation escaped to the West, but his family was sent to Siberia and we all ended up in the same settlement.

During those few days when the Germans were evacuating and the Soviet Red Army was approaching Tallinn, there was total anarchy. Some people escaped, some secured their homes and stayed there, some tried to drink themselves to death, some collected ammunition, and some looted warehouses and freight trains – all in the name of survival. Everyone was trying to figure out how to hide their life history. Estonian boys started returning from western Estonia, through the forests and on foot. Several came through our home in the city where we tried to help them with food and clothing. Aunt Elsa and Mother tried their best.

On 22 September the noise of battle lasted for some hours, but the front eventually moved through the city. The streets were totally empty of people. Along Paldiski Road a column of Soviet tanks drove in, witnessed by my aunt who was walking alone towards Lilleküla where she had been invited to help kill a sheep.

An amazing coincidence occurred on the last day of the hostilities in Tallinn. A misdirected cannon shot came through our window and just missed hitting the head of my brother, who had just returned from prison. The projectile came to rest, without exploding, in the oven. I was three meters away from it. Mother was also in the kitchen with the connecting door open. The force of the missile caused great confusion and disorder, with the air full of plaster dust and torn pieces of the broken window frame everywhere. Fortunately, all three of us made it out of the house.

In the chaos that followed the Soviet occupation, it was every person for himself or herself. A group of us discovered an entire train car full of military skis. Naturally, we carried

---

[6] The "Finnish Boys" were Finns who had volunteered to come to Estonia and to fight alongside the Estonians against the Red Army.[Ed.]

[7] Apparently the well-known author Jaan Kross had had a similar experience.[Ed.]

away as many skis as we could. A short while later, two boys from the same group (7-8 years old) decided to shoot off some rockets they had found. They didn't know how to handle the rockets, and one of the boys lost his hand in the mishap. It was a horrific sight – an eight-year-old bloody boy with his hand hanging from a piece of skin, staggering around with his eyes closed and muttering, "I didn't do anything..."

The occupation by the Red Army started what became known as the "Russian era." Our farm was given to the "new land claimers," the former tenants, for the second time. Later it became a part of a collective farm.

My mother and aunt were state employees and thus retained their jobs. My oldest brother became a plumber at Arsenal/Port/Franz Krull and studied in the evenings at Tallinn Industrial Technical School. Another brother attended the same school but was able to go full-time. The third brother, Paul, after finishing the Railway Technical School, also went to work while studying in the evenings.

Aunt Elsa took me by the hand to the second grade in Tallinn Secondary School No. 4 on Kevade Street. For the first two weeks of the school year we were housed in the Pelgulinna Primary School. My new school was a girls' school, and all teachers were nice elderly ladies, except for one male teacher who taught history. At first I did very well at school but then I became interested in other things. I started to wind yarn for Aunt Elsa's knitting and learned how to weave fabric, a skill I still have.

Mother was also using me in her moonlighting job. I was a living mannequin in the assembly of clothing. It was unpleasant and boring but I began to learn how to sew. Life thus went on until March of 1949.

Meanwhile, my brother Otto got into trouble with a group of technically minded boys at the school. With the approval of the authorities they took it upon themselves to restore an airplane. They got the plane running and even acquired a few liters of gas for a quick trip in the air. This apparently was against the rules, and the boys were all arrested, or "put inside" as it was called. Our home was searched and we were also in danger of being arrested. Most of the boys who fixed up the airplane were sentenced to eight to ten years at a labor camp. Otto got five years in jail and was sent to work on sea mines of Rõbinsk. They all did their time with the exception of a nephew of an important communist (Juliana Telman). He was soon seen walking around in the city.[8]

Mother began to send food parcels to my brother in the labor camp. I am not sure how she managed to do that. When she was baking bread for my brother, I remember hoping that some of the bread would burn and that I could get the burnt edges for myself. She also sent him other supplies, including clothes she made from pieces of fabric that came from old clothing.

Because of these parcels Otto was able to return to Estonia in a more or less healthy condition. However, when he got back he was not allowed to see Mother. The rest of us were by that time in Siberia.

In March of 1949 when the deporters came to arrest us and put us on the train, Mother was not at home because she had gone to Türi to her brother-in-law's funeral. This is how she missed the deportation train. I was taken, along with two of my brothers and my aunt. When Mother got back home, the guards had already left and the train had departed from Aruküla.

---

[8] The accusation apparently was that they built the airplane in order to fly out of Estonia and seek political asylum in Finland or Sweden.[Ed.]

There were 52 people in the train car, the youngest of whom was three weeks old. The mother of another baby had managed to hand her back to the grandmother. At Atchinsk the first five cars, including ours, were emptied of people (about 200 people) and their belongings were placed on the platform. We were then loaded onto trucks and taken along the ice road on Tchulym River to the district of Beleyusk. In the center of the town, horse-drawn sleighs met us and according to some plan, people were taken to different villages. Our family went to the village of Polevoi. We were shuffled into a hut that had a cast iron stove by one wall. Seventeen people were to share this room.

We were very lucky because my brothers were able to find jobs for which they got paid. With this money we could get flour mixed with chaff, we could buy or trade for milk, and occasionally get expensive potatoes. A hunger for bread has lived with me to this day.

A month later our family was given a small room with a Russian oven in the same building. The initial joy – sleeping on my own spot on top of the oven – turned into torture after a week. I found that the bed was too short and that I could not stretch out at night.

Aunt Elsa took me to the village school in Polevoi – a little girl crying and fighting all the way. There must have been an order to do this, because other children also came to the school. I did not understand anything that was said and thus did not take school seriously. I often played hookey, skipping class together with my friends and roaming about the *taiga*. When the school year ended I had not completed my work in sixth grade.

Student at Priiskovoye, 1949.

My aunt became popular with the Russians because she had had an education at the parish school and she could communicate with them.

Unexpectedly, the authorities ordered all Estonians to be settled in the autonomous region of Hakassia. We left on midsummer day, and it was a romantic trip. For three days we were on a barge floating downstream along Tchulym River, spending our nights by the fire on shore. We were given plenty of bread. At the Atchinsky train station we boarded a train headed towards Abakan. Half of us (including our family) were unloaded in Kopjovo, while the rest continued to Shiran.

We were loaded with our luggage on trucks and began our 100 km journey to our destination. We could see beautiful snow-covered mountain peaks. Our destination was the Priiskovoye Settlement in the Saralinsky District. The main industry was a gold mine and a gold recovery plant. There were three labor camps about five kilometers further up the road. Two of the camps had already closed, but the third one remained open even after we left.

Our family was assigned a small room at the end of long barracks – about 4 x 2.5 metres. It had a stove, two sleeping decks and a cross-legged small table. The fuel for the stove and the water buckets also needed to somehow fit into this room.

It later turned out that we had been very lucky to be assigned to this labor camp. Gold was an important strategic material and this mine produced a good supply of gold.

Food was available in the store. Even sugar could be purchased, and there was always a supply of bread. The store also carried fabrics like chintz, and heavy Russian overcoats called *puhvaikas*. Most importantly, we were paid for the work.

Despite the fact that the latitudes were lower than Estonia, the climate was like polar areas. Snow lasted for nine months. The sides of the mountain away from the sun were always covered in snow. We had to fit spring, summer and fall into three months, but we did it.

The season was much too short to grow any crops, with the exception of some potatoes. As far as I know, Estonians didn't even try to grow anything. There were plenty of berries, mushrooms and cedar cones in the forest.

Estonian friends, 1951.
I am in the back, right.

There was a strong wind, always from the same direction, and much precipitation throughout the year, with frequent thunderstorms. Average winter temperatures were -30⁰C, and sometimes even -52⁰C! The walls of our room were frost-covered and there was mold on the exterior wall. When the outside temperatures dropped below zero the condensed water in the room caused the single-pane windows to be coated with ice, sometimes as much as 10 cm thick. Transitions from summer to winter and vice versa happened overnight, no *ottepelei*.[9]

Road clearing was organized immediately because the more than two meters of packed-down snow could turn soft in a couple of days. The horses would then sink into the snow up to their stomachs, not to mention what would happen to the trucks.

There were no wells. Water was taken straight from the rapidly flowing stream and in winter from a hole in the ice; the water spot had to be sheltered by a tunnel many meters long and facing downwind. Lavatories had to be placed in areas open to the wind or else they would have been impossible to find under the snow.

---

[9] An extended thaw [Ed.]

It was very hard and exhausting for the workers in the mine. Nature had hidden the desired morsels of gold in a scattered manner in layers of quartz from 0.5 to 5 meters deep and mixed in other kinds of glittery minerals. Production technology was something like this: three shifts (6 hours each) would drill holes up to a couple of meters deep inside the quartz. My younger brother Paul did this job with a dry drill at first and ended up with silicosis for the rest of his life. Later wet drilling was used. The fourth shift was composed of the blasters who broke the rock apart. This work was done only by free people who were not under the control of the commandant.

Field trip with the Priiskovoye class, 1953.

In a couple of barracks-type dorms were exiled people from the Caucasus (*Mustad* [10] in Estonian colloquial language, based on the color of their hair). These were men who had been in the German army. Most of them were Armenians but there were also Azer and a few Georgians. They didn't exactly radiate intelligence, but with the lack of anything better some Estonian women used them as "teddy bears." "Look at him through my eyes," was one of the responses to the inevitable questions.

Ema Maria visiting us in Siberia. She is holding her grandson, Tõnu, 1954.

There were representatives of all kinds of Eurasian people. I went to school with their children for five years, at the Prooskovaya Secondary School. Maybe 0.5% of the students in the school were so-called aboriginals, or Hakassijans. One of these girls was in my grade. I was the only Estonian. The teachers were very good. They were also people with limited rights and came there under some category or other. Staff changed constantly. I later understood that even the highest bosses in the manufacturing complex could only stay there for a maximum of five years. They were then assigned to a new location, very far away.

The people who worked for the commandant did not have a right to travel. For example, my math teacher, a German woman, was very good in her field, but she stayed there after I left.

Some of the workers were prisoners of war. A load of German POW's arrived right after us, as well as some Japanese POW's, several hundred people in all. They were put to work in the mining operation. I did not personally have any communications with that

---

[10] Blacks. [Ed.]

Babylon of people. My friends were the Russian-speaking students who were very nice to me.

When I turned 16 I became an adult prisoner. I was ordered to appear at the commandant's office with a picture of myself. I was read my rights and ordered not to leave the area of deportation without the commandant's permission. A personal file was opened for me with the picture I had brought. This was later sent from Siberia to Tallinn to the Archive of the Ministry of Internal Affairs. When I saw the file 40 years later, I was surprised at how thick it was.

In September 1949 I went back to school to finish sixth grade. The construction of new row houses had begun, each with a kitchen and a separate entrance, built on pile foundations. Two years later our family was given one of these houses, perhaps because my older brother Felix was a very useful worker. Lack of skilled workers was and continues to be a problem in Russia.

Our new accommodations were nice, but I still had to share a bed with Aunt Elsa under the edge of her blanket in the small kitchen by the stove. It was warmer in the winter months because the outside wall facing the wind was frosted all winter long. The gaps between the logs were not insulated. But still, we had double windows! The room temperature was 5 to 12 degrees C.

Priiskovoye volleyball team. I am second from left

My brothers also slept in that room, and soon one of the brothers' living companions moved in with us. She had been on our train.

During the day when I was home from school, I was also in that room because the kitchen was Aunt Elsa's room for living and working. She was our cook, laundry woman, dressmaker and mender. Having had foresight, she had brought with her the Naumann sewing machine. Her skills had been developed at the Kehtna Home Economy School. She had also obtained a good pension from "Eesti Kodukäsitöö" (50% of pay).

Aunt Elsa was my guardian angel. I frequently moved under her blanket with the desk lamp. It was a good place for reading. My brothers had packed many books when we left, and from them I had learned to read Russian. I also used the school library, which was quite rich, especially in Western classics.

So the time went from year to year. I grew 20 centimeters in those five years. I looked like Twiggy, but unfortunately I was ten years too early and skinniness was not in fashion. Luckily, I was successful at school.

The schoolhouse was fairly close to our home and it had central heat. The school had a large walking hall where dances were organized. Dance practice was led by an old Jewish lady, a former theater dancer who had been fired from Moscow. She was good! She even directed the making of costumes. In some ways I was her favorite. I poured my fantasy into

Women students in first level, 1955.

dance. In Tallinn I had danced folk dance in Tombi for five years, and had attended the ballet school for a year, but I lacked the background and sense of classical music. At the district inspection we earned laurels!

The club house next to the school had a movie theater and sports hall. Even volleyball was played there, despite the low ceiling. The club showed a new trophy movie each week – whatever Russians had brought from Europe. It was said they were all later melted down to produce "good local cinematic works." The tickets were cheap and the cost was not an impediment. For some films, the teachers organized *oblava* [11] and of course these were the shows we all wanted to see.

The music at the club events was often provided by Estonians - accordion (school boy), piano (music teacher) and others. The gym teacher was a retired officer - drill, grenade throw, shooting - fun! None of this was difficult for me. I especially liked math, physics, and astronomy. My Russian grammar was at a high level, and in the seventh grade I was already correcting my desk mate's essays. She was a nice girl and I was her desk mate throughout school. At the math exam I solved everyone's problems behind the exam room door in order to raise the school's overall rankings.

In 1954 I passed the high school graduation exams. The teachers very much wanted me to go for

Priiskovoye graduates, 1956. I am in the white dress, front left.

---

[11] A round-up. Teachers would sweep into the theater in order to catch students who were forbidden from watching certain films.[Ed.]

a medal but that didn't happen. To me it was important to have a white dress. Aunt Elsa and I sewed it out of bemberg[12] and during exams I was embroidering the collar! I had the white dress but not the medal.

Again at the initiative of the teachers and without my participation, a member card for the Young Communist League was brought to me from the district center, 25 kilometers away, and I was given a very good recommendation.

From some handbook I had read about the mechanics-chemistry department of the Siberian Institute of Forest Technology in Krasnoyarsk, and this is where I sent my application. When I arrived at the institute, it turned out that the departments had been split and that my documents went to the mechanics department. This is how I ended up studying about mechanical treatment of wood.

I aced the entrance exams, getting 19 points out of 20, and passed the required level. There were 3.5 applicants per seat, and veterans' children were accepted without exams. I received a scholarship of 150 rubles a month from Aunt Elsa's pension, of which 100 rubles a month went for half a bed in a private apartment. My first living companion was Malle Vesilind, who was accepted to a different department at the same institute. Of our meager belongings we had one blanket to put under us and one blanket to cover us on a plain hard bed. Even then, it was possible to sleep, and we did not suffer for the lack of it.

That first year at school I was required on three occasions to participate in a "collective farm education." The first such work detail occurred right after admissions and lasted for ten days. The second was a few days after school started. We were assigned to groups and worked with strangers for a month and a half.

On the second work assignment I was with the daughter of a general – a real piece of work, but I got along with her very well. Our group consisted of two chemistry girls and three boys (I don't remember their majors). We were housed with some old lady on a collective farm. She received credit for work done in return for taking care of us, and she fed us as well as possible. We slept on the floor of the old lady's *izba*.[13] What was under us and what was over us I don't remember.

Our job was turning grain at a field several kilometers from the village. I remember it being burning, stinking, heavy, and endless. The weather was

Visiting with friends. I am back row center with hat.

miserable, but luckily, one of my group mates, a native of Krasnoyarsk, had loaned me a *puhvaika*.[14] Otherwise I would have frozen to death. My rubber boots were of little value because they had holes in them. I don't recall if we had days off. I do remember being drenched by rain and snow.

---

[12] A rayon made from cellulose, an inexpensive silk [Ed.]
[13] Traditional country log house [Ed.]
[14] A heavy overcoat. [Ed.]

My third summer job was a joy compared to the previous two. Our group of six girls was made up of our friends from school, familiar people with whom we had been to lectures for several months. Our job was hand-cutting silage. I liked the work and even learned how to sharpen the scythe. But the *mochkara*[15] and mosquitoes would have eaten us alive if the smart natives had not brought a simple remedy from the city – birch tar. (I don't remember what was used as solvent, possibly vodka or turpentine.) It did not matter that we reeked and had the appearance of Negroes. We were able to work in bathing suits in the sun. Too bad we didn't have cameras!

In my spare time during school I participated in the institute's dance group, took part in the volleyball practices with great enthusiasm (we had a very good women's team and a female coach) and went skiing. I had started to make contact with Estonians in Krasnoyarsk.

At the end of the first semester my scholarship was increased, but the second semester was ruined by the professor of Marxism, whose name I don't remember. He was a blind veteran who worked and moved about with a secretary (possibly his wife, very quiet, modest and pleasant). I am not saying I was very good in the subject, although I could write a good paper. As soon as the veteran realized that he had a deported person in front of him, he tried to destroy me. I could not get more than a "3" from him in my study record. I still received the summer scholarship, so nothing else mattered. My plans were to travel to Rudnik for the summer.

But once again fate interfered. I bought my train ticket, left part of my "treasures" with a schoolmate's parents and went to the commandant's office for the *spravka*.[16] There, without any introduction the commandant told me that I would receive a clean passport if I were to bring a passport photo. I told him my train was leaving that evening, so I could not get the passport in time. Only then I realized that a passport would be the only identifying document I could have.

I had to sell the ticket at the station and have a photo taken at the market. What made matters worse was that on the previous day I had had my long hair cut off and got my first permanent. But the passport was issued in one day, I think, and I still went to Rudnik.

When I came back to my family during the winter break, I witnessed many changes. A son had been born to my brother, the other brother had moved in with his future wife, and a cow had been purchased for the benefit of the baby. As it was hay time, there was suitable work for me in the hayfield, which was about four kilometers away. One day while I was in the field I saw a bear. There were forest fires – big ones. Even though there was no proper forest, the animals were on the move. Luckily they were not interested in me.

It was towards the end of July in 1955 when I heard that my mother, whom I had not seen since March of 1949, was coming to visit us. She arrived with an elderly lady, whose daughter and two grandchildren also lived in our settlement.

I don't think I was ever Mommy's "bundle of joy." Our age difference was 40 years and we had been living in totally different environments. I was not a source of problems for her and I also didn't need any advice. Mother had managed to dress me pretty well despite the difficult times, but she had also wanted to be the decider – to make me her "puppet." In my later life I wasted too much spirit and energy on things I didn't want to do at all, just to be a "good child."

---

[15] Black flies.[Ed.]

[16] A permission slip, in this case a travel permit. [Ed.]

68

A guest among her family, Mother enjoyed her first grandchild and then decided I had to go back to Estonia with her because I was "in the way" of my brother's family. I knew that Mother lived in a two-room apartment and that she had allowed several relatives to move in with her. My oldest brother, after getting out of prison, was also granted permission to live in her apartment. We certainly would have been in "each other's way". Mother also was not interested in having me continue my studies at the university but wanted to turn me into a "pants tailor!" The situation was depressing for me.

Eventually I gave in and agreed to go with her. I went back to Krasnoyarsk to take my documents out of school, not knowing what would come next.

I arrived in Tallinn a few days before the new semester began. Fate determined that things with school were to go smoothly. The rector of the Kopli School agreed to matriculate me, provided the dean would agree. The dean, Eugen Soonvald, took my documents, turned them in his hand for a moment, handed them to the secretary across the desk and said, "MM-31". I didn't understand what that meant but I also didn't have the courage to ask. I found out only on the first of September that it was the department of mechanics, the second year engineering group. A roomful of self-conscious young men and me – a girl from the forest.

Getting used to the new environment didn't go all too well. I was depressed for at least half a year. I never received the travel money because I didn't know that the State of Kreml was supposed to have paid for my travel back from Siberia. As I had one "3" in my study records (Marxism), I was left without a scholarship during the third semester. Tuition, which I think was 400 rubles a year, also was a surprise.

I sold my winter coat and with that money I paid back my travel from Krasnoyarsk. An old tenant lady on our farm gave me 1000 rubles as a gift. (She probably was feeling guilty because they had burned down the granary and the hay barn). With this I was able to live and to pay my tuition.

From the third year on there was no tuition. I did the obligatory month and a half of collective farm work with the girls from the economics curriculum. Among them were some of my schoolmates from elementary school who were very glad to see me. I started thinking about transferring to economics, but a boy from our group, who himself unfortunately failed a couple of years later, convinced me to give up that plan. Thus – over rocks and stumps – started my new studies.

Hilmo Seppel from Krasnoyarsk, whom I hadn't really known very well, joined my study group. We later worked together at the Tallinn Machine Factory but in different departments. We even played some sports together, including badminton.

I was full of energy and a happy girl. My nickname during those days was "Preili" (Miss), which fit me very well. My first name (picked out by my father) was not

Aunt Elsa at the 1969 Singing Festival in Tallinn.

useful. Even though it is Estonian, it means "empty place," and in Finnish it means "beer." After I got married my husband named me "Kiisu" (Kitty).

69

Graduation, 1959.

During my studies at the Tallinn Polytechnic Institute the dean, Eugen Soonvald, got all the students (including myself) of the engineering department a job at a business at ¾ time, i.e. 36 hours a week, which doubled the value of our scholarships. I was afraid that I would not be able to handle the job and my studies, but everything went smoothly!

After graduation I worked at the Tallinn Machine Factory. The current Song Festival Ground stage as well as the Kalev sports hall were constructed and built by Tallinn Machine Factory. I received a lot of help and experience from many "old" construction managers from the pre-war days.

Several senior builders went to work at the newly established Special Construction Bureau of the Academy of Sciences of Estonia, and half a year later they kindly asked me to join them. This was a most interesting job, which lasted for 15 years.

I had considerable trouble finding a living space. The department head almost managed to get me a one-room apartment in an old building, but the director gave it instead to a favored young couple. The department head's attempt to get me a dorm room also failed. Then I received the keys and address to an apartment at Mustamäe. Happily I went to unlock that door. Huge shock – some man had already taken over my room! Even being exiled to Siberia hadn't shocked me this much.

Finally, a friend, using his connections at the higher spheres of the Party, found me a co-operative apartment in Lasnamäe. The secretary of the Presidium of the Academy obtained the requested signature from the deputy president (I think it was Maamägi). I moved in September of 1980. The problem was the commute from Lasnamäe to my work; it was at least 1.5 hours each way.

The Technocenter closed down on 31 December 1991. I received a severance package that included four months pay. I was in charge of liquidation. I gave each man his drafting table and divided up the paper and drafting tools. Everyone took the chairs, tables, and cabinets according to his or her wishes. I allowed those who wanted them to take the technical library and books of standards.

I then got a job with the Ilmarine factory, where an Estonian affiliate of Finnish Nokia manufactured cheap gadgets for mobile phones. Several of my friends from Krull worked there. Hans Kuusik, my future husband, was the supervisor of the technical department. The construction work was done on a computer, in Finnish and English languages. I was at a distinct disadvantage and was put to work at the lowest level. It was a crummy job in a small room with no natural light. The business was then sold to another company and in the reorganization I and 42 others lost our jobs. Thus began my full retirement that lasts to this day.

I am trying to use this time of my life to do as many things as I can that bring me pleasure. For myself and my Krasnoyarsk friends I wish good health and a long, peaceful life.

70

Chapter 8

Kaljo Käspre

I'm my parents' only child, born on 14 August 1930. My father, Karl Käspre, Jüri's son, was born on 30 November 1902 and my mother, Katti Käspre (Hindrek's daughter) was born on 14 March 1904.

My father had a midsized farm called Uustalu in Väätsa, Järva County. Farm help was seldom used. From 1931 to 1936 my father worked at the Narva-Jõesuu station of the Borderguard of the Estonian Republic. He was a member of the Fatherland Alliance, the Defense League, participated in the parish activities, and was a member of the Väätsa Parish Educational Society. During the German occupation he was also a member of Self-Defense. Mother was a housewife.

This was probably enough for my father to be arrested in 1944 after the Soviet occupation. His sentence was 15 years in prison. He was sent to the north where he became ill with pneumonia and died in 1946.

My mother worked the farm by herself, and even made it possible for me to study at the Paide Secondary School in the late fall of 1944.

My mother and I were on the list of deportees for the 1949 March deportation because we were the family members of a bourgeois nationalist and thus untrustworthy and disloyal persons to the Soviets.

We were taken by train to Siberia, to the Novosibirsk region, Tcharnyi district, Krasnoselsk State Farm No. 266. Life there was better that it would have been on a collective farm because the workers were paid a regular monthly salary.

Local supplies of food were rather meager. The store carried almost no meat products.

In 1952 the Lond family, from our home district in Estonia, came to live in our settlement.

After the death of Josef Stalin in March of 1953, politics became more relaxed and certain relief of our living conditions could be felt. In the fall of 1953 we began our studies - Märt Lond, Erik Püüsalu, Ants Lond and myself. Märt Lond and I managed to finish grade 10 in the spring of 1954. Erik unfortunately didn't pass the physics exam. He passed it later, and thus our continuing studies took place separately. Ants still needed to finish grade 10.

Because Märt had studied at the Tihemetsa Forestry Technical School before the deportation, he did not need to think long about what specialty he would choose. He inspired me to follow in his footsteps, and thus I also applied to the Siberian Institute of Forest

Technology (Сибирский лесотехнический институт). Luckily we were both accepted. I took the exams to enter the Department of Forest Industry. After two years I changed departments and transferred to the Department of Mechanical Wood Processing.

Through the good offices of a relative, I was granted exemption from exile in 1956 and was free to move. I finished my third year of secondary school in the spring of 1957 and sent an application to the S. Kirov Technical Academy of Forestry in Leningrad. They accepted my application and I continued my studies in Leningrad. The move to Leningrad certainly made my life more interesting.

Students from Estonia had arrived in many colleges in Piiter (Leningrad). A young Estonian man by the name of Heino Pulk studied at the same academy with me. Through him we met Estonian girls who were studying industry trade. That's how we found our future life mates; I found Milvi Maiklik, who later became Milvi Käspre and Heino found Riina Veskus, who became Riina Pulk.

Friendship connects me to the Pulk family to this day. Unfortunately, Milvi died much too young in 1982.

After graduation I was sent to work at the Tallinn Piano Factory where I worked from 1959 to 1979, from 1963 to 1979 as the director of the factory.

From 1979 to my retirement in 1990 I worked as a department head of the ESSR Local Industry Design and Technology Institute.

I have two daughters – Piret, born 2 December 1961, and Katrin, born 17 June 1965, and three grandchildren – Andry, born 9 January 1981, Maria, born 10 February 1986, and Hanna, born 10 February 1996.

Chapter 9

Ants Lond

I was born on 14 June 1935 on the Koogemetsa farm in Karksi Parish, Viljandi County. Mother Linda died in 1936 of tuberculosis. From then until 1942 I was raised by Grete Jents, who had escaped from the revolution in Russia and lost her property. As the maid in a general's family, she had traveled widely in Russia. She was unusually optimistic and vital well into old age, and she lived to be 102. She loved to sing and had a wonderful memory, telling us many interesting stories about the days past. The love of her youth had died in the First World War, so she dedicated all her care to me. Aunt Grete's food parcels to Siberia were an essential help when, at the age of 16, I started my own life and later went to study at the district center.

Father Peeter came from a big family (nine sons, one daughter) and studied to be a tailor. In Estonia he had little chance to practice his skill, but in Siberia his profession helped us over the toughest times. His left hand had been shot through in the Carpatians during the First World War and that saved him from subsequent mobilizations. A couple of times, however, Father delivered military equipment to Lake Võrtsjärv, by horse.

It was a tradition at the farm to gather on Victory Day[1] at the flag pole and sing the Estonian national anthem. That moment has been carved in my soul, so that even now seeing the tricolor brings tears to my eyes.

Father married for the second time in 1942 to the farm girl Salme, who brought her parents Leena and Hans to the farm and later two half-brothers and two half-sisters.

We were saved from the 14 June 1941 deportation by the farm hand Juhan Priks, who had some kind of connections with the communists and warned us about the upcoming action. We hid in the nearby forest where there were already people from the village that we knew. I recall how native farmers were turning the knobs on the radio, hoping to find world condemnation for the evil we were witnessing.

After the Soviets occupied Estonia, they divided our 80 hectares farmland into two new farms. Our relationship with one of these families was satisfactory, but the thoughts and actions of the other one were based on the inevitable worsening of class differences. After

---

[1] 23 June. [Ed.]

the war he took part in searching for and arresting Estonians who were considered "enemies of the people". His life was ended by a bullet from a Forest Brother.

At the end of the war a former Russian POW Fyodor was brought to the farm to do farm work. He was treated as a member of the family. As he didn't much care for working, he was left to herd our seven or eight milk cows.

His freedom of movement was unrestricted, and soon he became a member of a communist partisan group. Twice they came to our farm and robbed it clean of food and clothing. The last time they came they even wanted to shoot Father but luckily he got away. The local constable was not as lucky; he was shot on a forest road. It's not known if the killing was that group's work.

After the war ended, Fyodor came to the farm for the third time, but he was no longer as militant as he was before. We did, however, still lose our bicycle. He probably thought that his harrassment of our family was a demonstration of his dedication to class struggle and was hoping for a lesser punishment from the Soviet authorities for falling prisoner.[2]

On the early morning of 25 March 1949 the room and the surroundings of the house were filled with soldiers. A young man named Tibar read the resolution of the Supreme Council regarding deportation of the peasant family and started to write down the assets. Our entire eight-member family was due for deportation:

1. Peeter Lond, age 58
2. Salme Lond (nee Oja), age 39
3. Ants Lond, age 13
4. Enn Lond, age 5
5. Rein Lond, age 3
6. Tiiu Lond , age 1
7. Hans Oja, age ca 75
8. Leena Oja, age ca 70

Half-sister Vaiki, the ninth member of our family, was born later in Siberia.

My half-brother from Mother Linda's first marriage, Juhan Seekõrv, heard about the deportation on his way home from Tallinn for the school holidays and had the sense not to come home. He stayed in Estonia but died in 1952 of blood poisoning.

I remember that we had finished meat smoking on the eve of the deportation, and we packed as much of this meat as we could carry. Our neighbor, coachman Hans Jõgimets, helped carry a big bag of beans and warm clothing to the sleigh. Grete brought warm pancakes to the Karksi-Nuia gathering point, and a classmate from the Nuia Secondary School (possibly Aime Allikvee-Pärnakivi) brought an algebra textbook. On the pages of the latter I wrote everything that happened in the cattle car, day by day.

It was a cold and clear spring evening when we were loaded on board an open truck. One of the guards sat next to the driver, and two soldiers with machine guns leaned their backs against the cabin that offered protection from the wind. They were very amused when their German shepherd tried to satisfy his animal instincts on the deportees.

---

[2] After the war the Soviet Red Army accused former POWs who had been taken prisoner by the Germans of desertion and many were executed. [Ed.]

74

At Puka railway station we were loaded into cattle cars with bunk beds built in. In the middle of the car was an iron stove and a stinking bucket for human waste. There were 49 people in the car when we started moving. The youngest was a one-year-old little girl and the oldest were an old couple, over 80 years old. The old couple died soon after our arrival in Siberia.

The door and the windows were closed, but once we had crossed the border we managed to open the iron shutters. At the front, middle and end of the train were soldiers with weapons ready to shoot. At the stops they formed a gray chain around the train.

Near Dno we saw a cow that had been harnessed in front of a sleigh pulling a load of brush. A genderless pile of rags in *valenki* sat on top of the load. At the time we could not guess that soon many of us would also be such emotionless eunuchs.

Around noon the train stopped. A few men were allowed to go for soup and to bring water and coal for the stove. This also provided the opportunity to exchange a few words with people in the next car, as well as to relieve ourselves under the car. The younger women were at first in a bind as to how to lift their skirts in front of the lusty eyes of the guards. But necessity really knows no laws, and towards the end of the journey one could see the opposite genders squatting while talking in a friendly manner.

The mood in the car was anything but fun. A large dose of optimism was instilled in everyone by Anna Juhkamsoo, the farm lady of Ruudiaru, who tried to convince us that soon the "white ship" would come and we would be allowed to return to our homeland with blue, black and white flags waving.[3] She sincerely believed that.

After being on the road for a couple of weeks, we reached the Tchanyi railway station. There we loaded our belongings on a big tractor sleigh for the 50 kilometer trip to State Farm No. 260. It was a very cold evening, and we warmed ourselves by jogging alongside the sleigh. We reached a heated schoolhouse by nightfall and slept on the floor. In the morning we were taken to the sauna where some sort of brown liquid was poured over each of us. Perhaps it saved us from some disease, but it did not prevent the appearance of lice. The locals did not consider lice a problem and were used to having them in their hair. It took several years before we were able to get rid of the lice.

Our eight-member family was housed in a room of about 20 square meters occupied by a then childless married couple. In addition to the "hosts," a calf also lived there behind the stove wall. The next day everyone was called to the office where work orders were handed out. Women were mostly ordered to care for and milk the animals, and men were sent to construction. After the snow had melted everyone was ordered to different farm jobs.

Around 1950 a man named Kask (who later turned out to be an attorney named Grossman) was brought to State Farm No. 260 of Tchanyi district of the Novisibirsk region. He organized all kinds of festivities, and during these he paid attention to everything that was said and all the songs that were sung and all the plans that were talked about. He gathered enough evidence to send all the men to prison camp for 10 to 25 years. Father had prior to that hit himself in the leg with an ax at a barn construction and was in bed at home and fortunately did not participate in the festivities. I can't remember if I had been there or not. A thorough

---

[3] The "white ship" was the hope that the Allies, especially Britain and the US, would not allow the annexation of the Baltic states by the USSR and would drive the Russians back, liberating Estonia, Latvia, and Lithuania. [Ed.]

search of all the living areas was conducted. While the search party was at the neighbor's living area, I managed to burn the journal I had been keeping.

Grossman's activities came to light when a jealous girl stole his report from his jacket pocket. After that he disappeared, presumably headed to new hunting grounds.

In the sumer of 1949 I gathered hay with oxen. In the fall I managed to continue studies in the fourth grade and finished it. The only "5" on my report card was singing. I was assisted by Juhan Juhkamsoo, who could not carry a tune himself but who wanted to sing even more because of that. He organized a joint singing of the song "*Läksin mina läbi küla tänava...*"[4] The song is about homeland, the schoolmate explained, stuttering a bit, when the teacher asked about the content of the song.

The next summer I could not study because most of my time was spent in herding 120 head of cattle. I enjoyed herding because I could read books borrowed from the teachers. In addition, I could secretly milk about 4-5 liters of rich milk to go with my bread ration (the amount may have been around 400 grams a day) or the sunflowerseed cake meant for feeding the cows. This was a big advantage that the fieldworkers did not have. Opening the silo wells in the minus 40-degree cold in winter, hayrides from the steppe and transport of manure were not exactly fun. We did it together with Kalmyk Maksim. Later I was also the water delivery person for the tractors, and for a while a construction worker and horse and sheep herder.

I am joined by my work brigade, 1956.

There were between 1200 and 1500 sheep in the flock. The barn built of sod was located 6 kilometers away from the village. It was quite warm in there in the winter, and I slept in the same room with the sheep.

The smoked meat we had brought with us lasted for almost a year. After it had run out, Kalmuk and I decided to kill a lamb. We figured that we could get away with it since no one could count the sheep as they were constantly being born and dying. So one stormy winter night we butchered a lamb and hid some useful meat under some hay. The rest of the carcass I put on the roof of the barn, in the snow. The wolves found it at night and dragged it to the steppe. Because such a deliberate action would earn a long prison term – a deliberate destruction of people's property by an "enemy of the people," I went tracking in the steppe for a couple of days in case someone came looking for me. Fortunately nobody seemed to care, but a vague fear remained and I tried to be more careful after that.

In the summer of 1951 I fell ill with malaria. I was in the same hospital room with a Korean who had been deported from who-knows-where and had the same disease. In between

---

[4] "I went down the village street..." The song is actually about a young man who sees a fetching young lass in a window and he asks her for a drink of water. It turns out that her parents have gone to the city, and after the young man has his water, she makes him stay in the house.[Ed.]

the bouts of fever I was very cold. When I regained consciousness I saw that the Korean man was trying to climb up the wall. I don't recall having tried that myself but I did have blood under my fingernails. After a week at the hospital I was so weak that Father had to carry me to the carriage. For many years after that I had to take quinine pills that Emma, an Estonian nurse in Russia, managed to get for me. The bouts of fever returned periodically, and a few times I fell off an ox or a horse when I unexpectedly lost consciousness. The symptoms finally disappeared after I'd finished secondary school.

I was generally of a weak physique and realized that studying would be the only way to get away from hard physical labor. When we were taken to the state farm center I altered my grade V report card by drawing one more line, making it grade VI, and thus made it to grade VII.

In the evenings I naturally had to work. We had nine people in the family then, and the only other person able to work was Salme. Father had by then become ill with brucellosis and was in very poor health.

With the final report card of grade VII, I was accepted at the Novosibirsk Distance Learning Secondary School. I had done all the required coursework, but I was not allowed to leave the state farm to take the exams. I added one more line to my Estonian language report card and went to see Malyscheva, the director of the Tchanyi Working Youth Secondary School. She was quite a smart and understanding woman. She patiently listened to my confusing story and issued a certificate for the state farm management to confirm that I had been accepted to grade IX along with the order that I be allowed to continue full-time studies.

Father was bedridden, but he gave me ten roubles and told me to try to manage, and that they would somehow make ends meet. It was very hard to walk those 50 kilometers to school, to walk with the knowledge that this may have been my last meeting with that smart and compassionate person. Luckily, even Father made it back to Estonia. Of our family only Hans Oja was buried in Siberia. Mart Kissa and his wife from the Rimmu area, as well as Peeter Aasamäe from Karksi predeceased him. Unfortunately I don't remember what happened to the others.

Erik Püüsalu and I at Tsanoi Evening School, 1955.

For a moderate fee I got a place to sleep on a window bench of a Russian family. My total possessions consisted of a backpackful of textbooks, a winter coat and work boots. Probably also a toothbrush. Quite soon and at different times Erik Püüsalu (from the senior year of Haapsalu Secondary School), cousin Märt Lond (from the last year of the Tihemetsa Technical School of Forestry), and Kaljo Käspre (senior year of Paide Secondary School) arrived to study. Arvo and Ahto Vallikivi, Kalju Nurklik, Mart Evert and a few others were already there as full-time students.

With Erik, Märt and Kaljo we found a place to live in a kitchen-room occupied by Nadya, a Russian woman with two kids. Nadya's husband was in prison. Space was tight. Erik and I slept on the big Russian oven, Kaljo and Märt slept in a single iron bed next to it. Nadya wanted to introduce Kaljo and Märt to her girlfriends but the boys were not interested. Regardless of that she was very proud of her tenants even though the rent was mostly symbolic. I have pondered a lot over whether an Estonian would have been as hospitable and as patient as she was. My later experiences make me doubt that.

The Vallikivi brothers lived in the next house, and that's how a group was formed that became of interest to the KGB. One evening Kaljo came, looking worried, sat on the bench for a while and suddenly announced, "Boys, I was recruited as a spy." A couple of days later the same was repeated by the more emotional Erik right as he came in. It was a sign of great trust and courage on their part and saved us from the worst. Grossman, the attorney, had lacked that courage, and because of him, many families in our state farm and elsewhere suffered greatly.

Writing weekly reports that were handed over to different contact people in different hallways was a rather interesting task for Kaljo and Erik. As recruited spies they were not supposed to know of each other's doings, and the reports had to be written with that in mind. That's how one report said that Märt was embarrassed because of his beat-up shoes and that's why he could not go dancing with the beautiful Russian girls, but that he hoped to make up for it once he learned a trade and started earning money. In the other, Ants or Erik would complain about the daily pea puree and were dreaming of a nice meal when all the proletarians had united and were happy at tables piled with food. It was essential to show awareness and add that it was necessary to work hard for the bright future as the main goal. It would be interesting to read those reports now and to find out how seriously they were taken by the communists. In any case, this kind of cooperation developed our imagination and lasted without hitches until we parted ways.

We earned money by doing odd jobs at the dairy factory and plank factory, digging canals and wells, and unloading coal from wagons. Sometimes we were lucky when we had to reload the boxes of chocolate, condensed milk, or spirits designed for the polar areas. These boxes had the admirable quality of dropping and falling out. There was a set expected percentage of loss, and we could not leave that unused.

Sometimes the local paper ordered short articles from me about the progressive combine operators and herdswomen. I remember the first line of one of my articles:

> Kombainjor Vassiili Rudnik ubirajet urožai s tridtsati gektarov v sutki, ještšo parenj, nažimai!

("Combine driver Vassily Rudnik harvests 30 hectares of crop in one day, go for more, guy.")

As a result of my article the young man became famous in the village. Once I had to show solidarity with him and had to drink a large glass of vodka in one gulp. It was not pleasant, and this experience did not inspire me to write other adulatory articles.

We spent one year together. Then Märt and Kaljo finished secondary school and entered the Siberian Institute of Forest Technology. Erik went to the Sports Technical School of

78

Novosibirsk. The Vallikivi brothers left around the same time. Over-exertion and malaria started to trouble me during the final exam, and so I made it to the Krasnoyarsk Department of Forestry with a two-year delay.

Many deported Estonians, Latvians and Lithuanians were living in Krasnoyarsk as well as descendants of the people deported during the Tsar's time. Estonians often organized spirited gatherings and celebrations. Common memories and the feeling of belonging, along with shared experiences, united the former students then and now.

When I got to Krasnoyarsk in 1956 some people had already been freed and had returned to Estonia. Still the majority were deportees and had to periodically check in with the commandant. One could leave the city only with his permission. That was probably the only demeaning fact we had to put up with. The boys were naturally free of military service, and we could use the time as we saw fit.

The level of the lecturers was surprisingly high. Quite a few of the teachers had previously taught at good universities. At the state farm we had at first been considered fascists. After that we became "kuraty" (kuratõ – kuradid – devils), but in Krasnoyarsk we were not set apart from the others. We were treated obligingly and with understanding.

I joined the Siberian song and dance group. The choir leader was a last-year student of the Vilnius Conservatory. In summers I was a worker under Märt, who had made it to the

Siberian Institute of Forest Technology 1956 graduates Kaljo Käspre and I. Looking out the window is Toomas Kodres.

position of estimator at the Aero-Photo Forest Management Expedition. The job location was in the *taiga* near the confluence of the Angara and Yenisei Rivers. It was hard work and we literally slept under a tree. We lived off hazel hens,[5] millet porridge, pea puree, and fish. The primeval nature was magnificent and the *taiga* and rivers full of game. We frequently saw rivers turned upside down by gold miners and villages abandoned by geologists. There was talk of piles of human bones near big rivers, presumably of prisoners who had escaped from the numerous gulags. In the immeasurable forest the rivers were for knowing one's way and for easier travel, but they also were well-guarded traps.

I once accidentally came upon a forgotten village of Estonians who had lived in Võrumaa. The only Estonian old lady left there told me about the post-revolutionary horrors that led to the extinction of this rich village, established during the Tsarist era. She said that this wasn't the only village that had disappeared.

I thought about the kindness that had been shown to us in Tchanyi by Nadya, the Russian woman with just a couple of grades of schooling, and the unthinkable horrors by the penal and

[5] Small grouse. [Ed.]

79

enforcement bodies that were promoted and justified by the communist ideology. I realized that the future could not belong to the communists. That kind of system feeds on itself. Germans were able to reevaluate their past. Will Russians do that? I don't know.

Our deportation ended in 1958 without permission to relocate to Estonia. The reason for that was not known.

My problems with the security apparatus resumed right after I tried to register myself in Estonia. I was told to leave in 24 hours, but with the help of good people I was given a year's extension. Either the times had changed that much by then or the officials were sloppy, but the issue was gradually forgotten.

I graduated from the Department of Forestry in 1961 and chose the field of forest improvement design. I have been working at this for 52 years now. In 1965 I married Ene (1939), who retired from her job as a doctor only this year. Our son Sander enjoys himself in the warm climate of the Mediterranean and is making his new home there. Grandson Peeter is graduating from Tallinn Technical Grammar School this year and will join the Kuperjanov Battalion for a year.

In summary I can say all is well that ends well, and with that, I close one of the chapters of my life.

Chapter 10

Märt Lond

I, Märt, Märt's son, Lond was born on 19 October 1930 in Mulgimaa, in Abja Parish, Pikasilla farm. My parents and my ancestors from both sides were farmers, and my childhood was spent on a farm. I had no playmates except for my sister, who was 14 months older than I. I started school in 1939 in the Abja-Paluoja sixth-grade elementary school. I spent the second year of school at the Karksi-Nuia elementary school because my parents had moved there in the spring of 1940. They had bought a second, bigger, Reiman farm near Karksi-Nuia. When the Moscow-minded government came to power in the spring of 1941, our family had to move back to Pikasilla, because the larger farm was nationalized and became a horse rental place for the new land owners. The following year of school I attended the Abja Secondary School. After grade seven I continued studies at the Forestry Technical School of Tihemetsa.

On 24 March 1949, around lunchtime, all the students of our year (we were in the final year) were ordered into a meeting and were told that we had to be ready to take part in some kind of action. All except for Märt Lond and Toome Andres. (Andres had been in the German army and his parents had defected to Sweden.) When we started to disband, our military teacher Jossif, an Estonian from Russia, stopped me and Toome and said, "You, boys, better go someplace for a while, it's better that way!" I had a bad feeling and hitchhiked to Abja to warn my parents, who had been declared *kulaks*.

I took the night train back to Tihemetsa and snuck into my accommodations at a nearby farm that was close to the Forestry Technical School. It was dawn, and having heard from the host that everything was peaceful, I went to my room and sat by the window where across the bare field I could see the school campus. I had decided to run if I saw any unusual movement. But for some reason the deporters had circled around the farm and approached it from behind.

When they came in, I had no other choice but to admit that I was Märt, Märt's son, Lond. Some kind of an order was read about deporting a person like me who was disloyal to the Soviet authorities, and I was taken in the same clothes that I was wearing. The hostess, a kind person, packed a bit of food for me to take.

That evening I started my way to Siberia along with my companions, none of whom I knew. Eighteen days later the train car doors opened at the Uzhur station of the Krasnoyarsk-Abakhan railway. From there we were taken on unusual springy wood carriages pulled by fast little hairy horses to the Kalinin Collective Farm in Temra Village of Sharypov District.

My parents, having learned of my capture, had returned home on the third day of deportation. Unfortunately, the deportation militia was waiting for them. They were sent to Dobrinka Village of the Tchanyi district in the Novosibirsk region, where we met at the end of 1950.

I lived in Temra for a year and a half. I earned my living in the collective farm and planned to continue my studies at the Sharypov Secondary School in the fall of 1950. That plan fell through.

Then I decided to move and to live together with my parents, At Dobrinka I worked in construction, leading a multinational construction crew until the fall of 1953 when I managed to get into the last year of the Tchanyi Evening Secondary School. I graduated together with Kaljo Käsper in the spring of 1954, and that same fall we became students of the Siberian Institute of Forest Technology in Krasnoyarsk, where about a dozen Estonians — companions in fate — were studying, as well as some Latvians and Lithuanians.

In 1956-57 the bulk of the deportees regained their freedom and returned to their homeland. I did not have that option. Partly because of this, Maie and I got married on 23 August 1956. Maie's mother and brother returned to Estonia that same year.

During my studies at the institute I was hired at the Krasnoyarsk Areo-Photo Forest Management Expedition as an estimator. My wife and I spent the summers in the *taiga*.

After my graduation from the institute in 1959 with a diploma of forest management engineering, in March 1960 we took the Krasnoyarsk-Moscow train, headed for Rakvere. From Rakvere we took a bus to Kunda, where Maie's mother, Armilde, lived at her parents' farm. Letipea had come to meet us with a horse and sleigh.

After the birth of our daughter Tiiu in Tallinn on 3 April 1960, we found accommodations near Karksi-Nuia. I did not have a permit to live in Estonia and had to go back to Krasnoyarsk in the middle of May. I was finally able to come to Estonia for good in January of 1963.

Abja-Paluoja, the capital of Mulgimaa, became our family's home, and this is where the two of us are now spending our

New Year's Eve party at the Railroad Workers Club, 1955-1956.

retirement. I worked as the supervisor of the Abja construction department of Viljandi KEK until the closing of KEK in 1992. Until my retirement in 2002, I ran the construction company A/S Abja Ehitus. In the early years of Estonian re-independence, when many farms were being reclaimed, I also spent a few years restoring my father's farm – Pikasilla. Our son Silver now lives on the farm.

Maie and I have two children – daughter Tiiu and son Silver, five grandchildren and four great-grandchildren.

Chapter 11

Rita Metsis

I was born on 15 May 1934 in Tartu. Father Jaan Aire and Mother Melita Aire (née Muri) were studying law at Tartu University. Father was from Laura village in Petserimaa that has now become part of Russia. Mother was from Valga. I was born together with my twin sister Tiia who arrived in this world fifteen minutes before me. On 27 August 1942 another sister, Una, joined us. After graduating from college, Father worked at the Tartu tax office while Mother raised the offspring.

On the night of 25 March 1949, the three of us – Tiia, Una and I – had to start the long road to Siberia without our parents.

Actually, the repression against our family started earlier on 14 June 1941. That's when our maternal grandmother who, after the death of our grandfather, had married a Latvian man and lived as a farmer's wife near Volmar (Valmiera), was deported to Siberia. They had owned a fabric store in Volmar as well as a productive farm, so the Soviet authorities had plenty of reasons for sending them to Siberia. The farmer's

Aire family, 1940.

two sons and a daughter from the first marriage, as well as our mother and her brother, were living elsewhere and were not deported. Step-Grandfather's children escaped abroad at the end of the German occupation and thus escaped the deportation, but they never saw their homeland again. The fate of Grandmother's children, however, was different.

Just as had been done in 1941, the deportation operation in 1949 included the separation of spouses. Often they were sent to different destinations. Step-Grandfather was sent to the salt mines in Solikamsk and no one ever saw him again. He could not stand the ordeal and died soon after arriving there.

Grandmother was taken to the Krasnoyarsk territory. After the war she wrote to us to let us know she was alive and well. And then, in the beginning of 1947, she miraculously managed to escape from Siberia. Mother's sister-in-law got Grandmother a fake passport with a different name. She lived under that name for the rest of her life.

Mother's brother was executed because he had been a member of Self Defense and had for a short time during the German occupation worked as an interpreter at Gestapo headquarters. Later, in the early 1950s, his wife was also taken to the other side of the Ural Mountains.

In the fall of 1941 sister Tiia and I started school in Tartu. After the war (1945) our family moved to Tallinn where we attended Secondary School No. 8 until eighth grade.

In the spring of 1944 Father was mobilized into the German army, which determined his fate and the fate of our entire family. With the return of the Soviets, a wave of repression hit our family in the beginning of March of 1948. After the war Father was working in Tallinn at the Ministry of Finance as the director of the tax office. He was arrested on 3 March 1948. The infamous troika[1] initially sentenced him to 25+5 years in prison, on the accusation of being a member of an anti-government secret organization. Malmre and Meriloo, members of that organization with whom he had been in the German army, testified against him.

Being a lawyer, Father could prove his innocence, but he was still not set free. Instead, he was sentenced to five years in prison according to article §58.[2] Mother got a letter from Father from Vyat camp in Kirov region where he was imprisoned with Estonians Heino Mandri, Eino Pillikse and Ottniell Jürissaar. They remained good friends until Father's death.

Mother wasn't home on 25 March 1949. It was school holiday, and Mother had gone to the country to get food from our acquaintances. Tiia and I stayed home to take care of our younger sister. At around three o'clock at night the doorbell rang. Tiia asked who it was. The building superintendent's voice was telling us to open the door for passport check. Right away a flashlight and a gun were aimed at us. A man's voice yelled, "Why is there no light on?" Several men, along with the superintendent, ran in and demanded to see the head of the household. Tiia said that since she was fifteen minutes older than her sister, she was the "head." A militia man read from a paper that, because we were the family of a traitor, we were to be deported. We were given an hour and a half to pack. One member of the militia advised us to pack newer and better things separately from the less valuable ones. We did not panic. We packed clothes, dishes, even a sewing machine. There were many pieces of baggage. We then asked if we'd be allowed to sing farewell. We got permission, and I sat down at the piano and started playing the Neapolitan song, "Look how the blue sea...," and Tiia was singing.

Our younger sister, who was six years old, did not want to get up or get dressed. One of the men said that she was a fussy child! It was about five o'clock in the morning. We were guided to the street and into a truck. The men brought the less valuable luggage out. The truck started, with the more valuable things left behind.

---

[1] A commission of three persons that issued sentences to people after simplified, speedy investigations and without a full trial. [Ed.]

[2] Article §58 of the Soviet Penal Code defined political crimes. It introduced the notion of an "enemy of the people." Those convicted under Article §58 were political prisoners, or *politichesky*, as opposed to common criminals. [Ed.]

Ülemiste station did not want to accept us without an adult, but our escort said they woud not be taking us back. With that, our things were tossed into the cattle car. We could hear complaints from those inside that there was no more room. When the car door was closed, it turned out that there was more room after all.

The car was pitch dark because the windows used for the animals had been boarded shut. Luckily there were some holes in the boards. When our eyes had become accustomed to the dark, we climbed on top of our bags and even pulled a few blankets over ourselves. There was much panic and tears. Older people, who had finally realized that they were being deported, were more upset than the younger ones.

The next day the train went to Aruküla station. We were hungry. We ate raisins that we had secretly taken with us. We had not been allowed to pack any other food. At the station the car door was suddenly pushed open for a count. Tiia managed to slip out. Somewhere close to the station building was a store full of people who all wanted to be served. Tiia asked to be able to skip the line to buy bread. The clerk immediately put several loaves of bread in her arms, along with several sausage rings. He wouldn't accept money. People in the line were crying.

The train started its journey east. Some time later the need for a toilet arose, and that was something the deporters had not bothered about. Someone contributed a bucket for that purpose, but the bucket quickly filled up and started sloshing over onto our packs. The stench was horrible! Someone had a saw and an ax, and a hole was cut in the car floor. During the trip the bucket was emptied into the hole as needed.

Once the train had crossed the Volga River, we began to get daily soup and bread at designated stations. We formed a food distribution group, and Tiia was also allowed out to bring bread. For our approximately 50 people, we were given two buckets of soup, two buckets of tea and five loaves of bread. That was the ration for the entire day.

There was little hope that we would see someone we knew. But then a rumor started going around that a mother was looking for her children. Because only five cars were allowed to go for food at the same time, it was not possible to meet the food carriers for every car and we were not able to substantiate that rumor.

One day, when we had spent a couple of weeks on the road towards Siberia, the car door opened at one of the stops and there we saw the face of our unrecognizably aged and grayed sweet mother at the door. It's not possible to describe our feelings of happiness and joy. Even today, remembering this moment brings back tears. Our entire railcar of peope were cheering.

In our car were also the old woman and man named Mandri – the parents of the actor Heino Mandri. They knew nothing about the fate of their son. They heard from our mother for the first time that Heino was alive, had been seriously ill and was with our father. We remained friends with the Mandris until their deaths back in Estonia. Also with us in the car were Anni Varma, Dr. Teemant, and Heli and Arno Susi with their mother.

A few days later the train was divided into two. We were taken to Krasnoyarsk territory and unloaded at Atchinski station. Our things were tossed onto a truck. By the way, Mother had managed to bring our better things with her. Having heard of the deportation, she had rushed home and found it ransacked. The half-drunk deporters had not yet had a chance to leave the apartment with our things. To Mother they said, *"Детки забыли"* ("The children forgot").

After the trucks were piled high with our luggage, we were ordered to climb on. The very rough journey along the "roadless roads" to the distribution center at Birilyus began. Along the way we were housed in a former church. The trip could only continue at night and on a horse-drawn wagon because during the day the warm sun thawed the road.

We came to the Tchulym River, where the locals were given an order to take the "fascists" across. The ice was melting and the river was no longer safe to cross. The locals worried that they and the "enemies of the people" would drown. Finally, with great reluctance, they were persuaded to take us across the river.

Somewhere along the way it was decided to treat us for lice. As we at that time didn't have lice yet, the treatment was inapproriate.

After a few days we were taken to some abandoned huts in Polevoye Village. The windows of the hut we entered were boarded shut, but one small window still had a few glass squares. We prepared beds for ourselves from what we had brought in our baggage. It was already April, and the nettles and wild leek had started to grow. We could trade with the locals pieces of clothing for potatoes and onions.

Tiia's recollection of the house in Siberia.

Next day we were taken from the village to burn huge grain fields that had been left unharvested the previous fall. The fire was lit at several locations. Wild animals ran out, including many mice. The field was burned clean "for purposes of fertilization" and for sowing new crops, as dictated by the controlled economy. At the same time, there was a grave shortage of bread! We were given a quarter of a small loaf of bread a day. No money was paid for work.

During the following days we were taken to work at the grain silo, to the fields to plant something, and to the *taiga* for forest work. Tiia and I, two 14-year-old girls, were given a two-meter, two-man saw, and we went to the forest with the others to cut down trees. We were told to cut down a big larch.[3] At first we could not do it. After that we had to cut into sections those trees that others had cut down, and then we had to split the sections for firewood. This wood was used as fuel for the trucks. That was hard work. We were later sent to shovel and stir grain at the silo.

In the beginning we had to fight hunger. We traded clothing for a pregnant cow who was supposed to give birth around midsummer. She was a pretty black cow and she became our pet. We acquired a hatching hen that hatched out twelve chicks. We dug garden beds behind the house, made furrows, planted potatoes, onions, carrots, and beets. It was June. The weather was hot and beautiful. We started to settle in.

---

[3] A large conifer common in colder climates. [Ed.]

86

In the morning of Midsummer Eve, when many people had already been sent to the forest several kilometers away, the commandant came and told us we would be taken away in a few hours. Pack your stuff!

It was once more like deportation. We could not bring the cow and the chickens. Tiia went to the local Latvian neighbor lady, who bought our cow for ten rubles. She did not have any more money. I got eggs for a chick; the mother hen sealed the deal. Three egg-laying chickens were cooked and taken along for food.

I had a hard time helping Tiia kill the chickens. I just could not hold them down. Finally Tiia said that she could do it herself and that I should run to find Mother.

I ran into the forest to tell her what was happening. I did not want to lose her for the second time. Tiia pulled up potatoes that had already sprouted and packed them in a bag. She hung our freshly washed laundry on the line, and this dried quickly in the breeze.

Mother arrived in time. We were loaded on a barge and the

I'm not of much help, as depicted in sketch by Tiia.

tugboat started pulling us along the Tchulym River. Hordes of mosquitoes were attacking us. People were swelling up. Our dear mother was waving a kerchief all night over her children's faces to keep the bloodsuckers away. During daytime the mosquitoes hid and Mother could sleep a little. In the evening we were allowed to eat and sleep on the shore of the river. We had tasty cooked chicken and potatoes that we could bake over the fire.

From the barge we were taken to a gold mine. Able bodied people without small children were taken higher up in the mountains, to Pryiskovo, while mothers with minor children were sent to the abandoned mining barracks at Verka to please the starving bedbugs. Bedbugs were falling on us – crackling. They were translucent. Our great war against them included using boiling water and kerosene.

The gold mine.

Siberian nature is beautiful and rich. Red and black currants, raspberries, strawberries, blue-berries, and wild leek grew in the forest. Beautiful flowers like peonies, lilies, and cyclamen-like flowers were sticking out their noses even at the edge of the permanent snow. During thunderstorms it was as if we were in the middle of a battlefield, but no one was hit.

Tiia and Mother went to work at a gold mine that was being closed down because there wasn't much gold. I will explain the gold mine according to Tiia's description. Tiia was sent to work the pump that pumped the water out of the mine. The engine of the pump was so spent that it was throwing out sparks everywhere, but obviously Tiia survived. The water pumped out of the mine went into troughs along with the gold sand. Under the watchful eye of an armed guard, women used scrubbing brushes to wash the sand in the troughs. There was a sieve underneath and the gold dust fell through it. The sand was pushed on with scrapers until it fell into a hutch and was taken away from the mine.

In reality the mine looked like a big gravel pit. In Pryiskovo, where the younger families had been taken, a different production method was used.

There was very little gold at the bottom of the trough - 20 to 100 grams a day. It probably wasn't pure gold but nevertheless the workers were not allowed to touch it. Soldiers with machine guns received it in a sealed box and took it away. People were warned that, if they managed to find pieces of gold, they would immediately have to hand it over to the shift supervisor. If it became known that someone had kept any gold, they would get 20 years in jail. A piece of gold looked flat like a grain of oatmeal but smaller.

Instead of a salary we were given coupons called promissory notes. About ten of those were given and we had only a month to "buy" goods from the store with them. The trouble was that the store was almost always empty of goods, and the locals always rightfully cut in front of us in line. If we had not been given a bread ration by the commandant, we would have seen bread only in our dreams. For four people in our family we received one loaf of bread.

The store sold cocoa powder in big, 25 kilogram paper bags, and sugar was sold in large lumps and loaves. At the end of the month we inevitably had to buy those items without coupons.

In the fall we went to school. In time, people began to treat Estonians better as they began to understand that we were quite tolerable, not bandits.

We had procured for ourselves the necessary winter clothing - including the cotton-filled coat *fufaika*. The Russians had *valenki* and foot wraps. It wasn't possible for us to get those. So we had to get through the winter in Põhjala rubber boots.[4] Luckily we had woolen socks and we could in addition use woolen foot wraps. But outside it was cold, around -40⁰C. The coldest it got was -57⁰C.[5]

Tiia got very sick with pneumonia. The doctor who came at Mother's call said Tiia would not make it. Mother wrote to Father in Vjatlaager, and Father got some medicine from Heino Mandri, who was working at the camp's medical unit, and sent that to us. That and some miracle helped Tiia get back up in a month. She fell ill before Christmas, and did not go back outside until grass was starting to grow.

---

[4] Rubber boots that would be called Wellingtons in England. [Ed.]
[5] Minus 70 Fahrenheit! [Ed.]

We had an iron stove in our barracks. When that went out, frost took over again. Water in a glass left by the bed froze and broke. After that a hot water bottle was put under the covers. At night, big rats attacked everything. Mother tied the bags of groats[6] up under the ceiling, but the rats managed to jump up from the floor and tear the bags open. Sometimes the rats ran over the bed.

Because of Tiia's sickness we were allowed to move from the middle of nowhere to the center at Gidra. Later on we moved to Ordzhonikidze, closer to the railway. In time, the other families were also given permission to move away from Verka.

And then came the time for Father to become free – 3 March 1953. Two days later the world was also freed of Stalin. Father came to join us as he had "honestly done his time." We, however, had still been exiled to Siberia forever.

The same year – 1953 – I graduated from secondary school and started studies at the Siberian Institute of Forest Technology in Krasnoyarsk, initially in forestry, and from second semester on at the Department of Chemical Treatment of Wood. Unfortunately I was not allowed to study at the Tomsk Polytechnic Institute, even though I had an invitation from them to study there.

Aire Family, 1953.

For two years we lived in a basement apartment and studied with Juta Vilk (Siirak). We were modest and progressive students.

On 14 May 1955 our forced exile came to an end. From the release papers we found out that we had been deported according to an order dated 1 October 1949, which had been issued seven months *after* the actual deportation! Great – wonderland, Russia!

The family returned to Estonia – at first sister Tiia, then me. It was a wonderful feeling to cross the Estonian border. Could I really be home again after a forced absence of almost seven years? A few months later Father, Mother and younger sister Una also arrived in Estonia. At first we lived in Pääsküla, which in those days was Harju County, as we could not get residency registration in Tallinn. We managed to move to Tallinn in the spring of 1957.

Starting in 1955 I studied at the Tallinn Polytechnic Institute as a transfer student in the Department of Chemistry and Mining, from where I graduated in 1958 as an engineer-chemist-technologist.

I started work at the Silicalcite (later Silicate Concrete) Institute established by Johannes Hint and worked there for 35 years. It was interesting work with many official trips all over the Soviet Union from Vladivastok to Lvov and from Tbilisi to Norilsk. For many years I gave lectures at the Moscow All-Union Institute. For a while I was also a doctorate student, but unfortunately I did not defend the thesis.

When the Soviet Union disintegrated, the Silicalcite Institute also disintegrated. My work there came to an end in 1992.

---

[6] Whole grains of various cereals. [Ed.]

For ten years, 1993 to 2003, I worked at the Sunday School Community of the EELK,[7] established by Juta Siirak. My work there was of a technical nature – working on the computer, typing texts, paginating, and designing books and journals.

In 1961 I married Ivar Kisper. At the end of the same year, on 20 December, our son Ivari was born, and on 29 April 1963 our daughter Ima-Riina was born. In 1966 Ivar and I divorced. Ivar passed away in 1993.

In 1983 son Ivarit married Eha Vannaasseme. On 23 June 1984 their daughter Jaanika was born – my first grandchild. Jaanika now also has a family; my first great-grandchild Sten-Marcus was born on 10 January 2005.

In 1996, daughter Ima-Riina graduated from the Department of Medicine at Tartu University in the field of nursing. For years she worked as a lecturer at the Tallinn School of Healthcare. In 1998 she married Aadu Hint. And two feasts for eyes are growing – Katharina Salome and Aleksander Oliver.

Father left us on 25 January 1976 and Mother on 30 March 1989. Mother got to see the blue-black-and-white flag on top of Tall Hermann. My dear twin sister Tiia died on 5 January 2010. With her I had shared the trip to Siberia, and her memories are included in this story.

Adi Metsis and I were married on 15 May 1999. The wedding took place at the Harju-Madise church and was conducted by Juta Siirak, my friend from Siberia days.

Every year we get together with the Estonians who studied in Krasnoyarsk. I hope these gatherings will continue until even just two former Krasnoyarsk students remain!

Life goes on!

---

[7] Eesti Evangeelne Luterlik Kirik (Estonian Evangelical Lutheran Church). [Ed.]

Chapter 12

Allan Onton

The calendar showed 8 September 1931, when in the dining room of Rajasoo farm in Servaääre village in Kohtla Commune in Jõhvi Parish in Viru County, with the help of a midwife, the male population of the planet was increased by one unit.

By then, the roads and fields of the area had been walked on by at least eight generations from my father's side. But the fate and direct influence of these generations on my own life and fate as a person is probably indirect and difficult to perceive; more influence can be measured in verbal messages that reached me from my grandparents, but unfortunately only through my parents. Being the youngest child of aging parents, I never met any of my grandparents.

My father August, born in the fall of 1881, was the second son in a family of peasants. He described his father Kaarel as a calm and typical peasant. Hard field work had not brought Kaarel riches, however, and his health deteriorated after a horse kicked him in the chest. He eventually had to hand over the wallet and the documents to the farm to August, his barely 16-year old son. The first son Johannes, a couple of years older than my father, had already chosen the trade of a craftsman and refused to do farming.

The young master, despite his lack of education (parish school and half a year in the so-called ministry school) turned out to be energetic and enterprising. With the help of acquaintances who had moved to St. Petersburg, Father established ties with shopkeepers and restaurant owners there. He started a potato business by sending potatoes from his farm and the neighboring farms in a rail car to St. Petersburg. The transactions were successful, which led to his almost life-long attachment to growing this crop. He even earned the title of local "potato king."

All his life he had an unusual peculiarity that repeated itself in my own youth. Namely, we could not eat. Or to be precise, he could not swallow any kind of meat, no matter how it was prepared. No, we weren't some fanatical vegetarians, but nature had coded that taboo into us. In addition to that, Father was a teetotaler until the age of 37.

The first critical years of his life were 1905 and then the years of the First World War. In 1905 he was elected into the revolutionary Kohtla Farmers Union, and because this was considered a revolutionary organization, he was in danger of being shot by the Tsar's troops.

During the revolt of 1905 many manor houses were destroyed, but since the local manor house had not been burned down, my father escaped execution. He did, however, spend many weeks in the basement prison in Toompea Castle in Tallinn.

He was drafted into the Tsar's army and was attached to an armored car regiment in Kuramaa, and later in St. Petersburg in the Putilov factory working as a semi-free soldier on the production line for packing cannon projectiles. His worker's number – 45 – was so etched in his brain that when he was absent-mindedly sitting with a pencil in hand, the number would appear on the edge of the newspaper, or on a calendar, or on some other paper.

During his St. Petersburg era, in the village of Estonians near Luuga, he managed to make the acquaintance of a girl fourteen years younger than him – Pauliine Kepper. The acquaintance developed into a friendship and then love. The young couple married at the Luuga Lutheran church in 1918. They escaped the whirlpool of confusion in Russia during the Bolshevik revolution and made it to August's home farm in free Estonia. During the 1919 elections for the Estonian Constituent Assembly, he was elected in the farmers' list as the delegate for Viru County. So he temporarily had to settle in Tallinn, where in 1921 my older brother Ilmar was born, their first child. After the parliamentary elections Father returned to the home farm, continuing to promote the growing of seedling potatoes.

In 1925 a daughter was born to the family, my sister Ingeborg. According to Mother, she was an angelic child — beautiful, good, calm, and smart. But as it often happens, God calls good people to Him early. That also happened this time. In the fall of 1930 acute appendicitis took Inge away. Perhaps this was God's will to save her from the worries and evils of this world that soon fell upon our land. At least that is what my mother thought.

In 1931 I arrived as the third child. It's highly possible that I was meant to be a substitute for my sweet sister who had departed the year before. Perhaps the appearance of another boy did not bring great joy to my then rather mature parents, but I cannot complain of any lack of affection. Neverthless, during the first years of my life I was frequently dressed as a girl in memory of my sister.

Being the youngest child on a relatively rich farm meant a carefree and safe childhood for me; the main danger was excessive pampering. But on a farm parents don't have too much time and opportunity to dedicate to a child or to buy him expensive toys or candy. Some of my caprice, however, was accepted. At a few years of age I still walked around with a pacifier in hand so that I could dip it in sugar and then suck it. This had apparently been called *"kahtam tuuts."*[1] Then there was my categorical refusal to eat rye bread. I had to have white bread exclusively. Add to this my distaste for meat, which required the preparation of special meals, and it is clear that I must indeed have seemed quite pampered.

In 1941 all this easy life changed dramatically. We escaped the 14 June deportations because we were far away from home and no one came to get us. When the war started on 22 June, militiamen came to get Father, but he managed to get out of the window and to hide himself under currant bushes. I was supposedly playing in the yard, but I took him word that one guard had been left in the house and that he should wait for dark and to not come home. He then hid himself in the next village in some old people's farm. Brother Ilmar was an active Forest Brother in a bigger group in Võrnu. Only Mother and I were left at home.

On 15 July, a month after the deportations, the chairman of the executive committee of the parish, rifle in hand, showed up in our yard, and with him was an armed group of several

---

[1] A childish game [Ed.]

dozen men – a subunit of a Latvian destroyer battalion.[2] Machine guns were set up at the edge of the road. Mother and I were commanded into a car while the search, destruction, and devastation of the house began. This lasted for several hours. We were then driven to the Kohtla-Järve military base where we spent the next 24 hours, after which I was taken to a crossroads and asked if I could go to some relative's place. I was ten years old, and that's how my first imprisonment ended.

Mother stayed at the military base and we did not hear from her for more than three years. In the fall of 1944 we received the first letter from her. Up until then we had believed that she probably wasn't alive and was one of the nameless corpses that were frequently found along the road.

My path to education had started at the Kohtla elementary school in the fall of 1939. The school was located in the former manor house, not a very fancy one. I finished three grades there (two grades in the second year – the second and third grade in one additional year).

In the summer of 1941 the buildings of Kohtla Manor and the nearby settlement – Kohtla-Nõmme – were completely burned down by a destroyer battalion. At the beginning of the German times schooling continued in the so-called firehouse, and later in a barracks-type building. In 1944, as the Red Army was moving back into Estonia and the front was approaching, this building was taken over by the army and was used as a military hospital. We received our sixth grade report cards in the beginning of March in the principal's apartment.

Everything was lacking in the school of those days; we folded our own notebooks out of brown paper, and we made ink by mixing soot with water. Pencils and books were scarce.

In the spring of 1944 I graduated grade 7 from the half-burned Kohtla-Järve Elementary School, which used to be one of the most beautiful schools in the country. I continued my secondary school education at Kohtla-Järve, riding my bicycle almost seven kilometers each way. Here students developed lifelong friendships and close ties that persist to this day. We continue to meet in different places all over Estonia every year.

The composition of the class became peculiar in grade 11 when several "boys" who were six years older and who had served in the Russian army joined us. They had been given the opportunity to receive the "right" secondary school diploma since several of them had the "wrong" diploma, i.e., a German or an Estonian diploma. Among them were future leaders such as Heino Kaljuste[3] and Valdo Pant. The latter had to interrupt his studies for health reasons. While he was a student, Kaljuste was also our music teacher, and Pant was our art teacher. Regardless of this anomaly the atmosphere was friendly, understanding and supportive. Unfortunately, none of these "boys" are any longer around.

Having made it to the last grade with the first graduating class of the school in 1949, my studies were interrupted when on 25 March my father and I were deported. We were put into a small cattle car No. 1 of a deportation train where 17 people like us were already gathered; the oldest was a 75-year old lady and the youngest a two-month old infant. In front of us was a bigger car No. 0 with about 50 people in it.

---

[2] Destroyer battalions were groups of paramilitary personnel, formed by the communists during 1941 as the German army was approaching and the Red Army was withdrawing. The battalions usually consisted of about 12 men who were sent into towns and villages to bring fear and terror to the population. They had total free hand to murder, pillage, and destroy. [Ed.]

[3] Father of Tõnu Kaljuste, founder of the Estonian Philharmonic Chamber Choir and popular choir and orchestral director. [Ed.]

Of the trip to Siberia I remember only isolated events, such as the train stopping in Jõhvi for almost a full night and day where letters were written and dropped out through cracks in the door near the railway crossing. It later turned out that the majority of the letters made it to the addressees.

We started getting food and hot water – *kipjatokk* – on the third day of the journey. Before we got to the Ural Mountains only women were allowed to fetch the water. We also got some thin porridge that was distributed in buckets. The men were not allowed out of the cars. The first time we were allowed out of the cars was in the Kungor station in the Urals. I remember seeing kiosks selling jewelry and objects made of gemstones.

In my memory and my mind's eye there's a unique and degrading image: the train made a pit stop going through the Urals. Everybody was chased out of the cars onto a slightly sloping clearing to relieve their natural needs so that they wouldn't soil the railroad cars. The clearing was filled with people of both genders, in different poses and positions. Disgusting perhaps, but in some ways also darkly humorous and surreal.

As the trip progressed we arrived at the Atchinsk interchange station where our train turned south; the sun was shining and we were allowed to keep the car door open. The journey from Atchinsk lasted for almost a day and night, and then we came to the end of the trip – Abakan. There the travelers were chased out of the cars together with their bags. The directors of the collective and Soviet farms in the area were at the station to meet us, and there they then selected their "slaves." Our carful caught the eye of the collective farm "*Za kommunizm*"[4] directors Jenin and Kuzmin. There was also an old man with a rifle who appeared to be a security guard. He was a veteran of the civil war and had a long, gray beard. Perhaps they noticed that we had three young men (the other two younger than I) and a young woman with an infant. They failed to notice, however, that the rest of the car was made up of old people with not a single able bodied man among them. In any case, we heard later that the other collective farm directors gave our new masters a hard time for having made a poor choice.

From the Abakan station we were moved by trucks a few kilometers to a river by the same name. The ice on the river was already brittle. The trucks were stopped, the bags tossed on sleighs that we ourselves had to pull across the river. On the other bank the bags were reloaded onto waiting trucks. The journey continued over the more sturdy ice surface of the Yenisei River.

The next morning (8 or 9 April) we arrived at the district center Karatuz, about 120 kilometers from Abakan. This village had three collective farms, although in 1950 they were joined together into one large farm. Two or three more railcars full of people from our train were also sent there. From car No. 0 came people from Jõhvi, including Harri Teever.

A sort of housing took place; all the people from our rail car had to fit into half of a so-called five-walled house. We were allowed to take a sauna and to rest.

The next day a group of us was taken about eight kilometers on a wagon across the mountains to a place where the local people of the collective farm lived during the entire sowing season and later again during grain harvesting season.

We were housed in one room that had one cot. Everyone slept mingled together. Cornmeal was our food; hot water with a splash of milk added was called tea. Every day a food deliverer came from the village. In the mornings he would bring the brigade members

---

[4] Translated as "For Communism." [Ed.]

94

milk-bread from their homes in the village, and distribute drinking water. I was sent black bread that the locals did not want to eat; their bread was similar to whole wheat bread. Rye was practically not sown at all and grain was limited to spring wheat and corn.

There was no way to wash ourselves and so we were soon covered with lice. I eventually got rid of them, with the help of my great aunts.

While I was at the farm my beautiful blanket disappeared, and I had to cover myself in bed with a coat. In the beginning I did not even have an adequte coat, so my clothing was insufficient for the weather.

My job was to assist the tractor driver and to hook up the towed devices. I was a collective farm worker while the driver worked for the tractor station. A day's work for me was calculated on the basis of some percentage of the work effort. We got paid with a few hundred grams of wheat grain in the spring and straw for each calculated work day (*trudoden*). Since there was just me and my rapidly aging father, our food table was rather meager. Fortunately we had brought from home both flour and semolina. Families with women gladly helped us. We were especially grateful to Auli Palm, who had been brought along with her sister's two small children (3 and 4 years old) and with little else. There was also Kristiina Supp, a 75-year-old farmer's wife from our village, who had given birth to twelve children. She was deported along with her daughter-in-law and a two-month-old baby.

The situation in general was rather poor and depressing. We were assured at the fortnightly inspections that we had retained all the rights of a Soviet citizen, with the exception of the right to leave our location. So Harri Teever and I decided to start studies at the local secondary school. That apparently was not a problem. We elected to attend grade 9 of the local secondary school. This way we would not become final year students right away. Back in Estonia in the Jõhvi school Harri had been in grade 9, and I had almost graduated from grade 10.

Chess tournament.

Now we were desk mates in the last row. I can't say that we were treated poorly. At physical education we were among the best. Slowly our language skills improved so that in the spring I received the complete report card. Harri, however, didn't have a grade in Russian, so he could not complete the grade. He chose not to study further right away.

A weird experience with discrimination in sport occurred during my schooldays. I participated at the district local chess championship and with one round to go I was in the lead. Inexplicably, I received a visit from the local prosecutor Kozlov, who until then had been the district chess champion. Now he was in second place after me. He told me that the party committee had decided that I should intentionally lose the championship match to him the next day, since I would not be awarded the first place anyway, regardless of the outcome. Of course I didn't agree to that and did not give up my first place. I asked the gym teacher for his opinion, and he tried to find out what the story was from the department of education. The response apparently was unclear. I won the match, but the district paper announced that there had been a championship with 14 participants and that the winner was Kozlov.

A few years later (possibly in 1952) something similar took place at the territory level. I traveled to represent the sports society of our district *kolhoznik* at the territory chess championships, and this time I was not allowed to play, ostensibly because I did not belong to the sports society *Urozhai*. Here the organizers may have been correct, because by that time I had already left the collective farm.

I left the collective farm as the result of an all-state campaign to raise poultry production. In Karatuz the incubator and poultry-raising buildings were being built a half a kilometer away from the village, near a cemetery. However, there was no workforce and that's why the commandant received the order to transfer men from the special exile to do this "shock construction."

I, with my meager work experience, was included in this group. At first we put up log constructions for the main building and the local power station which housed two motor-driven generators to ensure an uninterrupted power supply. Meanwhile, together with the old gentleman Johannes Kalter (who, as I have since found out, was the recipient of the Cross of Liberty[5]), we built about ten Dutch-style brick ovens to heat the rooms. (I found out later that they were not very effective!)

Our own house in Karatuz.

---

[5] "Vabadusrist," a medal of honor awarded to soldiers who fought in the Estonian War of Independence. [Ed.]

When all that was working, I became a salaried hatchery worker with a title of mechanic-electrician of the power station. Work was seasonal, and when we were working, we worked in three shifts. I had a considerably high degree of responsibility, especially for a guy like me. When we were operating, we consistently had over 10,000 eggs in the incubators.

The hatchery season started in the end of April and ended in July. The complex was led by a man named Filimonov, a party hack, and a manager named Klyukovkin – a younger man with special training, to whom all the call operators reported. All the operators were women.

I observed the work of the hatchery as well and made mental notes, so that a couple of years later when Klyukovkin left, I offered myself as a replacement. This is how I became the chief of the hatchery.

Once in charge, I changed the tracking mode a bit and positioned the grates and relocated the incubator, resulting in a dramatic increase in hatching. The success rate increased from 54% to 75%! We became the winners of the all-Soviet agricultural exhibition. I couldn't, of course, travel to Moscow, but the prize – 500 rubles – allowed me to think about further education.

There had been a political thaw since the death of Stalin in 1953. Harri had his grade 7 diploma. We could both go to study at the Krasnoyarsk Athletics Technical School. I started inquiring as to whether or not I would be able to follow the example of comrade Vladimir Ulyanov[6] and pass my final exams as an external student. The school wrote a letter of support to the territorial department of education, but I also needed permission from the Ministry of Education. In any case, in the spring of 1954 I passed the exams and received my diploma.

The hatchery work crew, 1955.

By then all our family members who had been sent to prison camps and to exile had all gathered in Karatuz. Mother got out of Kemerovo camp on the exact day that her ten-year sentence ended – 15 July 1951. In 1954, my brother came from the Kazakhstan camp.

Now it became possible for me to try to get into a university. I chose Tomsk and the major with the highest stipend as my goal. This was a mistake since, as it turned out later, the chemical synthesis field was classified and I had no chance of being accepted. But in actuality

---

[6] Lenin. [Ed.]

my exams also didn't go too well. I was offered an opportunity to study coal mining but I turned that down and went back to my job in Karatuz to apply again a year later during my holidays. This time I applied to the Siberian Institute of Forest Technology in Krasnoyarsk where I knew there were no political obstacles.

I have lifelong memories of the days at the institute. The commandant of the dorm was an understanding man who added me to a room that already had two men my age: Karl, a man of Polish origin who had been deported from Latvia in 1941, and a Latvian named Pavels. They were both applying to the Department of Mechanics. Understanding and friendship were born among us that exist to this day, even though we can only visit Karl now at his grave in Ventspils, where Pavels and Karl's brother, Stefan, now live.

We could live at the dorm only only during the admission exams so we started to look for a place to rent together. My choice of major, wood chemistry, was once again based on the value of the stipend. The admission exams went well and I resigned from my job.

I was introduced to the Estonians of Krasnoyarsk by Harri. I quickly got to know two Estonian student girls, Õilme and Ipe. I remember a grand gathering of Estonians in an unfinished building where the Estonian construction group men worked. The 1955 New Year's Eve was wonderful. The great political "thaw" had reached Krasnoyarsk!

There were also memorable parties for the smaller circle – with the Õunapuu family or at Peet Treikelderer's place. Peet had an apartment next to the institute.

One memorable party with Krasnoyarsk Estonians.

In time, the "thaw" also started melting away the Estonian gang. The Kuusemaas were the first to leave, and then one after another left. But there were also newcomers to the institutes. For example, now the Pedagogical Institute was available to people in special exile.

My studies went well and so did my chess game. There were no more special clauses. I was mentioned by name even on the poster for the territory championships.

But success also had its downside. On one spring month in 1956 I was called to the personnel department of the institute where I was introduced to a pleasant looking man who claimed that he knew me. He expressed his wish to meet with me soon at his room, No. 120 at the Hotel Sever. I had a hunch what this would be about, but I didn't know for sure. Times were changing, after all. I went to the meeting and heard many good things about myself. Apparently I was well-respected in scholarly circles, I had nerves of steel and a will at the chess table, and so on. This litany followed, naturally, the proposal to work for the KGB. I was offered monetary compensation and possibilities to travel abroad. It was stressed that all the staff were new, that the "criminals" who had deported people like my family had all been swept away, and that the special exile would soon end.

My refusal of the offer was not accepted. Instead I was told to give it some more thought for the next six months and then we would meet again.

We did meet again in the same hotel, in the last half of October 1956, during the Hungarian uprising. This time it was quick. If no, then no. You can see what's going on and your assistance would be helpful. You are wrong to refuse, but nothing bad will happen to you. You just have to sign to confirm that you will not reveal anything of these meetings. With certain relief I gave my signature, and until the new winds started blowing I really didn't tell anyone of what had happened, at least not in detail.

Amnesty for our family was initially delayed. In the spring of 1958 I received the notice that I was free of the special exile and could get a Soviet passport from the passport office. Mother and Father got their exemptions at the same time, but my brother did not.

The family together again after 13 years, 1958.

I sent an application letter to the Tallinn Polytechnic Institute asking them to accept me as a transfer student. I received the acceptance letter signed by the rector, Ludvig Schmidt. The Siberian Institute of Forest Technology did not put up any impediments. Quite the opposite. They made sure I would not have to take any additional prelims or exams at the new school, and they entered into my study record all the subjects offered at polytechnic institutes during the first three years. My thanks to those people.

In July I traveled to Karatuz for the last time in order to start on the way home, together with my aging parents – first on a truck to Abakan. Then, after a big argument at the ticket window, we received train tickets to Moscow. Finally, on 28 July 1958, we arrived in Tallinn, where my father's sister Pauliine lived with her daughter and son-in-law, who had in 1957 returned home from Norilsk and married my cousin here.

The first group of Krasnoyarsk Estonians to return home,
with well-wishers.

We were received well, and I managed to get my documents to the TPI in time. Father and Mother soon went to our home village and settled at the farm of Father's other sister. As our house had become part of a Soviet farm, my parents had to be tenants for quite some time – initially in Kohtla, later in Jõhvi.

My brother's exemption letter arrived in 1959. By then Lehte from Võrumaa, his love from the camp, had gone to visit him and they had married.

I stayed in Tallinn as a boarder with my aunt. My cousin, who had graduated from the Department of Economics, had many single female friends, and in 1959 Vilma Taal changed our social status from single to married. The contract is still valid and there are two generations of descendants: daughter and son, and they in turn have two boys and a daughter, whose books of life are in the beginning stages.

My new major at the institute was engineer-technologist, in industry branches dealing with organic chemistry. Studies went well, and my classmates were nice and accommodating, even though I was somewhat older and had been politically marked.

I graduated from the institute with honors and was referred to work as a designer at RPI Estonian Industrial Design. I stayed there for 25 years. I guess the job fit me and I was good at it. At first I was a simple engineer-technologist, a few months later a team leader, then the deputy department head, and for the longest time – altogether for over 20 years – a project manager. In 1985 I left government work and joined the project team for the Kirov Fishing Collective Farm, also as the lead engineer of a project. In 1988 when one could smell the Soviet Union burning, our daughter, niece and my wife joined me on a sightseeing trip to Krasnoyarsk and Karatuz. It was interesting to see everything again: the dam and power station at Divnogorsk, Pillars, the favorite location of mountain climbers, and broader Karatuz with plank roofs replaced by slate.

The annual reunions of the Krasnoyarsk Estonians have been delightful. For how much longer, I do not know, but I hope they will continue.

100

Chapter 13

Karin Rammulus

This is one of many similar stories (some sadder, some less so) that people who have felt the fear and pain of having been occupied by a foreign power carry with them.

I, Karin Rammulus (née Õunapuu), was born in Tallinn on 14 January 1931. The doctors had ordered Mother to give birth in Tallinn due to medical reasons.

My grandfather Juhan Veidrik (7 March 1863 - 1944) was born in the Väike-Maarja Parish, Porkuni Commune. He worked at Rägavere parish Põlula Manor. That's where my mother Henriette-Helene, Juhan's daughter, was born on 2 March 1902 to a farmhand's family as the second child. Grandfather was sent to work at the cattle farm of Männikuvälja, which is where Mother spent her childhood. This is where she finished the Ministry School and later the secondary school in Rakvere. In 1925 she finished the postal-telegraph-telephone course and began working as an official.

In 1928 Mother married the Virumaa County telegraph-telephone net mechanic, Johannes Õunapuu. Two children were in our family, my sister Ethel, born 28 October 1929, and I.

My father Johannes Õunapuu was born in Virumaa County, in Haljala, in Tatruse Village in a small Õunapuu farm that was 27.2 hectares, 13.6 hectares of farmland and 10.3 hectares of forest. The family had three children: my father, his brother and sister. Father's brother was already dead when I started remembering things; Father's sister was a good and caring aunt whom my sister and I often visited in Loksa. Grandmother Ann Rakvere and we spent Christmases at Tatruse, where the tree was decorated with long candy in colorful wrapping, and where we took Christmas bread to the animals and rode to church with the sleigh bells ringing.

My Rakvere grandmother Liisa Veidrik (9 June 1887 - 25 November 1966) was Grandfather's second wife. My mother's mother had passed away when Mother was little. Liisa Veidrik became our grandmother and the best grandma ever.

In 1918 my grandfather Juhan Veidrik bought a plot (1820.9 m^2) and a wooden house in Rakvere (3 Lossi Street). This was nationalized in 1945. In 1995 the land was returned to us, and we received compensation based on rehabilitation. My early childhood, happy and carefree, passed here in this home.

My childhood home in Rakvere.
At the gate are Grandfather and Grandmother.

In 1938 I started going to Rakvere First Elementary School together with my sister Ethel. I finished in 1944. Schooling took place during the war, and we had to move to a secondary building. After finishing elementary school I attended Rakvere Secondary School No. 1 where I studied until the spring of 1949. I consider the school years happy; we had nice teachers and a friendly class. In my spare time I took part in the school's gymnastics team, and we also went to the Tallinn Olympiads.

Villi Rammulus was in the same class with me. A class behind us was Endel Rammulus, the school champion in skiing, whose picture on the honor board was known to everyone. Villi left school in 1946 when their father Eduard Rammulus was arrested. Eduard Rammulus was sent to a prison camp where he died in 1947. He had been a member of Self Defense, fire chief and a store owner – thus a traitor.

The boys' mother, Paulina Ross, was born in Poskuni parish on 6 December 1899 as the third child of farm owners Mari and Jaan Ross. She married Eduard Rammulus on 26 December 1921 in Väike-Maarja.

After leaving school, Villi became the breadwinner for the family. He worked as a clerk at a clothing store in Rakvere. He was deported to Siberia in 1949 from his home in Rakvere. Fortunately the boys' mother Paulina was not home when the deporters came, and thus she stayed in Estonia.

I was sent to Siberia with my mother as a member of a *kulak's* family. My sister Ethel

Rakvere grade 9 class.

had been in Tallinn when the deportation occurred and was left behind.

Tatruse Grandmother Ann Õunapuu died in 1939, and the farm was left to my father. Because we were living in Rakvere, Father had hired a maid to work at the farm. In the evenings she would also do some farm work. Using another person's labor made my father a "kulak" who had to pay high taxes to the state. In the summer of 1949 Father was arrested for not paying the taxes and was sent to forced labor in Käva II mine in Kohtla Järve.[1] Father was released in 1952 from the mine but then was sent to join his family in Siberia. It was a small consolation that Grandmother could stay behind.

Our journey began on a truck, then in a cattle car. The rail cars were located a short distance away from the Rakvere station. People had gathered there prior to departure, including my classmates from whom I received the last farewells. I still have an old notebook in which I made notes during the journey:

26 March 1949: we woke up at 6:30, crossed former Estonian border into Russia.

28 March 1949: we were given our first water and food.

29 March 1949: we were allowed out of the rail car.

1 April 1949: Sverdlovsk. Urals have left me with a very nice impression. Many trains with the deported stopped on the railway sidings.

4 April 1949: Left the train at Petropavlovsk. In Omsk met a long train from Latvia.

4 April 1949: Novosibirsk. Went to the station to buy food.

4 April 1949: Heading south to the Altai Mountains.

8 April 1949: Abakan – final stop. From there on trucks through Minussinski across the river, then full day and night at the Altai Mountains. In Upper-Ussinsk housed in a secondary school for the night.

11 April 1949: Head count and slave market. It was confirmed that we had been deported for life.

12 April 1949: All have disembarked about one kilometer away; only the people from our car are pushed 5 kilometers m to the Tenyochkino village on the collective farm *Вперед*.

14 April 1949: We move on with five pairs of horses because the roads are bad. We are given an old renovated office building for living in. Sauna in the evening. We do odd jobs cleaning up litter in the fields, cleaning grain, etc. By the end of April Mother and I are put to herding sheep. Our collective farm is pretty decent as the majority of the inhabitants are *kulaks* deported here in the 1930s from Russia and Ukraine.

20 June 1949: I receive first parcel from Father in Estonia. I send letters and wait for letters. Mother and I are watching the herd – sheep replaced by pigs. The barns are about a kilometer from the village – former old farm buildings. Going to work in the morning is like a fairy tale – the woods and mountains are filled with flowers of all kinds, especially the peonies.

31 October 1949: Three Estonian girls – myself, Beate Kask and Lina Joonuks – go to grade 9 of the Upper-Ussinski Secondary School. I get a place in the dorm.

---

[1] A town east of Tallinn and west of Narva on the coast of the Gulf of Finland.[Ed.]

Here Mother and I were herding pigs. (my drawing)

In 1951 I finished the Upper-Ussinski Secondary School along with the other Estonians. I was living at Beate's at the time as Beate's father had got out of prison to join his family and they were given an apartment. We were free of the collective farm and the brutal work. Beate and I, nicely dressed and carefree, would walk on the Ussinski boardwalk. The principal of our school was a progressive man who recommended that right after finishing school, we should continue our studies in Krasnoyarsk.

High school graduates, 1951. In the back row, first left, is Linda Joonuks. I am second from left, and to my right is Beate Kask.

I left behind in Ussinsk the first great love of my life – Endel Rammulus. Many dance parties in secondary school and at the club, common gatherings – that's how it started and that's how it remained. Villi's and Endel's lives were more difficult than mine. They both herded horses in the mountains, and Endel later worked on a tractor. In the evenings he would earn money playing the accordion and was one of the founding members of the local Estonian band. Eventually Endel managed to fight his way out and come to study in Krasnoyarsk.

In 1951 I took the admissions exams to the Krasnoyarsk Medical Institute. Despite my good grades, the mandate commission did not pass me due to my deportee status. I also tried with the forestry institute but there, too, I received a negative response.

The question was – what to do – go back to the collective farm? Beate had already made the decision to go back. I decided to keep looking.

Finally I was accepted to the Krasnoyarsk Athletics Technical School. I stayed in the city, found an apartment and started my studies. I graduated from the technical school in 1953. Part of the time I lived with Õilme Mesila (Vilder) and Ipe Kobina (Vernik) in an apartment.

In 1952 Endel made it to Krasnoyarsk after finishing the Upper-Ussinski Secondary School and was accepted to the Siberian Institute of Forest Technology. Many Estonians were in the city. My father had been sent to join us. Since I was already studying in the city, Father was able to stay in Krasnoyarsk as well. He was given a bachelor apartment in a dorm and an electrician's job at the factory. Now Mother also joined us from the collective farm.

Our apartment in Ozyornaya on the banks of the Katša River became the permanent gathering, partying, and dancing place for young Estonians. We were all young, happy in our way, and in love.

The three of us: Õilme, me, and Ipe.

Endel moonlighting.

Our home in Ozjornaja, on the shores of two rivers.

Birthday party for me (25) and Hilmo (24).

In 1953 I started working at the Krasnoyarsk Medical School as a gym teacher. The school treated me well and the students were nice. Among them were many Volga Germans who were especially nice. In the fall I went with the students to help out at the collective farm. The roads were almost impassable, muddy and bottomless. The work was like a stage play performed at night with lights. I worked at the school until 1957.

On 12 April 1956 I was rehabilitated along with others who had been deported without court order. I was given permission to return to Estonia. Most of the Estonians went back in 1956.

First Estonians return home, 1956.

Endel, however, had not graduated. He applied for a transfer to Estonia to the Tallinn Polytechnic Institute. He received a conditional positive reply. If he finished the year, he would be accepted. In 1956 we went to Estonia on holidays to find a place to live in Tallinn while he was studying. One of Endel's relatives, Jete Kaal, had a house in Pääskülas and promised to help us. On 2 August 1956 Endel and I got married in Rakvere. After the holidays we went back to Krasnoyarsk.

We returned to Estonia in 1957 with our little daughter Sirje who had been born on 16 February 1957. I remember the following incident from the return trip: Endel got off the train at the Novosibirsk sta-tion to buy milk. The train pulled away, leaving Endel behind. I told the conductor what had happened, and at the next station the baby and I, along with our luggage, were left on the station platform. People helped me carry my things to the station building, where I waited for the next train that brought Endel. When he arrived we got back on another train. That episode extended our trip home by three days.

We came to Tallinn because Endel already had permission to continue his studies. Sirje and I also got permission to live in Tallinn. My mother, however, didn't get such permission, even though my father had died in Krasnoyarsk.

Endel, Sirje and I lived in Pääsküla and I got a job as a dorm mother at the Tallinn V. Klementi City Trade School. Soon we got a small apartment in the same building as the dorm in Pronksi Street. After graduating from the institute, Endel got a job as an engineer at the Norma factory. Some time later we got an apartment in Mustamäe.

In 1962 I started distance studies at the Department of History of Tartu University, graduating in 1968. From August of 1968 I worked as an assistant to the principal of the City Trade School No. 15. In 1969 I began work at the V. Klementi Trade School as the assistant principal and later as the dean of studies, until my retirement in 1986. In 1978 I was given the Honored Teacher's Award of ESSR.

Endel worked as the assistant technical director of equipment in Norma until his retirement. Our daughter Kaia, born in 1971, graduated with a master's degree in mathematics from Tartu University

Sirje, Endel and I going home, 1957.

in 1995 and now works as the comptroller at NG Investeeringud OÜ in Tallinn. Kaia has a partner, Eno Salumets, and they have two children – Marin and Marten.

From 1976 to 1979 Sirje studied biology at the Tartu State University but she did not graduate, transferring instead to the Räpina Gardening Technical School where she graduated in 1985. She was the 1996 Estonian champion in floral arrangements. Sirje has two sons: Taavi Varm and Leevi Varm.

I have been retired now for over 25 years. Endel died in 1997. I took care of the summer house Endel and I had built in Tornimäe, Laulasmaa. Now the children take care of it. I live in Tallinn, the carefree life of a grandmother and a great-grandmother. Would I have wanted to change anything in my life? Probably not.

Chapter 14

Hilmo Seppel

It's sometime in March 2013. I am still in bed, but I am bugged by the obligation-agreement I made with my Estonian/Siberian friends: each one of us has to write down in free form the story of his or her life. I had just finished writing and publishing my book *Illinuku Lugu*[1] which took me a year and a half. Am I ready to start a new project? But this is different, I tell myself. This is for all of us. This collection of memoirs will remain as a memorial to our life in Krasnoyarsk. So here I go.

The story of the Seppel family is an exemplar of the lives of most Estonian people — divided into two main parts — with the first part ending in 1940. The era before 1940 has been saved in memory as "the first Estonian Republic," politically a relatively stable twenty-year passage in people's lives when their standards of living and education were in constant rise. What followed was totally different as the small Estonian nation was in a painful way caught in the powerful millstones of history.

I will begin with the first part.

My parents, Miina Tõsine and Albert Seppel, were born at the turn of the last century. Their fathers were "forest captains," which means that in addition to farming they also had to employ themselves in seafaring to support their families. Grandfather on

The Seppel family, in Saaremaa, 1940.
Hilmo, Father, Mother, Vello, Simmu, and Uno.

---

[1] "Illinuk" is a nickname for Hilmo, and "Lugu" means story. [Ed.]

Mother's side would carry spa mud to Pärnu and Riga, which provided him a pretty good income. Grandfather on Father's side would haul rocks from the sea for the construction of the Tallinn port. This income stopped with the end of the Tsarist era. Mother received a good pedagogical education at the Valga Seminary. Father finished the parish school and continuously raised his qualifications with different pedagogical courses. Thus they were officially recognized schoolteachers.

Their work as teachers began in 1916, already in the Tsarist era. Mother was at the Muhu county ministry school and Father taught at a village school of Pihtla County on the island of Saaremaa. They married in 1925 and transferred to the Leisi school, at that time Saaremaa's biggest school. It eventually developed into a real center for education and culture. Miina and Albert Seppel were honored and valued teachers and revered members of Estonian society.

Human life starts at birth. To me that happened on 13 March 1932 at the Leisi schoolhouse.[2] At home, three brats were already waiting for me – Mother and Father had already had Uno, Simmu and Vello, with just under two years between all of us boys. I was the youngest of the family, and now I am the only surviving brother.

The family was large but our parents' state salary was sufficient for normal life. In addition to that, for many years we had our own cow and pig in the barn. My parents were also assigned a small plot for growing vegetables. We also had a hayfield, so there were enough chores and housework for all of us.

Life's work – going to school – started when I was seven. The word "go" is not quite accurate, because our family lived in the schoolhouse, in the apartment provided for teachers. However, I had to change schools seven times before finishing high school, and I never attended the same school for more than two years in a row. This "dance" with schools started in 1940, at the critical time in the lives of many Estonians.

The attraction of literature caused my father to leave his job as a teacher and go to work at the "Estonian Publishers" in Tallinn. Then the war started; Father was mobilized into the Soviet Red Army and was to go to Leningrad. But they did not make it to Leningrad because German planes damaged the ship so badly that it could not continue. Once back on shore, the Germans treated them as soldiers and Father was put in jail. He got back home to Saaremaa on Christmas Eve 1941.

The new German-controlled government would not give Mother a job at Leisi School. As a former Red Army soldier, Father was also unable to get a teaching job. The first year we lived in Pamma and the next two in Eikla. The family's financial situation had drastically worsened but Father did all he could to improve the situation. He started keeping bees, which later became his second profession, and we grew tobacco in the garden and this sold well. The wool carders[3] that we manufactured as a family were in special demand.

In 1943 the Germans arrested Father again. He had committed no crime, and he was released on the condition that the next day he would become a German soldier. Instead he went into the forest and intended to escape to Sweden. The plan was to hire a launch that would bring our family out of Saaremaa. That plan failed when a storm swept the Baltic Sea.

---

[2] A typical schoolhouse in those days included living accommodations for the teachers. [Ed.]
[3] Carding is the processing of brushing raw or washed fibers such as wool to prepare them for the weaving of textiles. [Ed.]

In 1944 Russian rule began, and Father was arrested for the third time. His crime apparently was that the Germans had not shot him. A couple of months later he was free again. From then on we lived in Leisi, not in the schoolhouse now but in a red house.

The next big change in the life of our family was very sad. Brother Vello was arrested in 1947 for having "decorated" a poster of Stalin with a hanging rope and the slogan, "Proletarians of all countries, unite!" Two years later that became the reason for our family to be deported to Siberia.

That day – 25 March 1949 – was a fateful day for 20,000 Estonians. I was a student in the tenth grade of the Kuressaare Secondary School, but it was spring break so I was at home in Leisi.

There were rumors of deportations and so my parents sent me to hide in the attic of the neighbor's barn. When the deporters came they asked where the boy was. Both of my parents claimed that they didn't know where I was. The militia deporters did not believe them and suggested that they call for me since I would be captured anyway. It would be wiser for the family to be together, they said. So I came out of hiding. We gathered the things we considered useful and sat in a car under the guard of gunmen. I remember how the journey took us downhill from home, towards the town. I was waving my hand at our home and thinking that in no more than ten years I will be back. As it was, I was back in seven and a half years.

The travel destination was Jaagarahu port where a big cargo ship was waiting for us, the hold of which was accepting our companions in fate. We were trapped in the hold for three days. The next destination was Paldiski. There we were reloaded into big rail cargo cars that had sleeping cots at the ends, and in the middle a tin oven and a bucket for natural needs. These conditions are described by many other deported people. The journey lasted for two weeks. The first time we were given food was in Kingissepa, on the other side of the Narva River. We were given bread and some kind of porridge or soup. The food was sufficient and we were able to save the five or six loaves of bread we had brought with us.

We arrived at the Korzhula station, 300 kilometers before Novosibirsk, where a "slave market" was held. This, too, has been described by many participants. The value of our family was high in the eyes of the "shoppers". Father and Mother

Our own house in Balman, 1950.

111

were 50, relatively young, and I had recently turned seventeen. In addition to that my parents spoke Russian and I had also studied it for five years at school.

Balman village in the Michailovsk district 60 kilometers north of the railway became our new home. Several families from Leisi parish settled there together with us. A few days later we were put to work. Father was given an ax and was told to build a barn for the animals.

Mother didn't have to work at the collective farm during the years in Siberia, which was a great advantage for our family. My first job was bringing half-rotten bottoms of hay piles for animal feed from the steppe with oxen. I worked with a local boy. Later came harrowing fields, haymaking and grain harvesting. The fields were four to five kilometers from the village, and some of the workers slept on cots in the barracks built in the steppe, men and women together. The other building was a cafeteria. At noontime on Saturdays we were transported back to the village, where we could wash ourselves in the sauna. Then back again on Sunday.

Driving oxen, 1949.

The first year in Siberia was full of work and worries. Potatoes and vegetables had to get into the ground. Those who had the money bought a cow (300 rubles); Father and Mother also bought a house (300 rubles).

Our family lived relatively well. We received food parcels from home, sent not only by relatives but also from the parents of former students. Heartfelt thanks! In general I would say that the Seppels were lucky in life. Good luck may be our fate but there is also definitely a heap of wisdom and activity and a lot of work.

Life continued like that until fall when we realized that I had eaten all my pay and some of Father's as well in the steppe cafeteria. The problem needed a solution. A bunch of Estonian boys attended the tractor driver's course at the machine-tractor station. Their pay was much higher than mine, and I was probably facing the same fate.

Mother was then the one who walked 30 kilometers from Balman to the district center in Tchumakov, where the only secondary school of the big district was located. She needed answers to three questions: do I have the right to go to school, will the school accept me and where would I live. All these questions found positive answers. Then it was my turn, on the last day of August, to walk the 30 kilometers to school.

I went to the ninth grade which had approximately ten students. In addition to me, Estonians Valter Velvet came to school to grade 7, and Leonardo Laesson to grade 10.

During the summer I had managed to learn the spoken language. I wouldn't have thought written language to be so different. I began learning grammar and memorizing new words. At school we were each day given four or five pages of text to read. On each page I found many new words. There was a dictionary but finding words in it took time. Mother, whose knowledge of Russian was perfect, helped us when she could. That's why we used her as a living dictionary during the weeks at home. School was hard but we managed. Two years later I was at the top of the class in Russian.

It was the spring of 1951. Now what? Deportees like us could not go to university.[4] Fortunately the principal offered me the job as the school librarian. I could not have imagined anything better. My pay was also important to my family economically.

I also became involved with musical groups. My parents were very musical and this rubbed off on me. I could play keyboards, the accordion and the piano. I could carry a tune and I knew how to read sheet music as well as any Estonian youth going to secondary school.

Thus went the first four years in Siberia for me and my father and mother. Now briefly about my brothers.

My oldest brother, Uno, after finishing secondary school, served in the ancillary services at a German airfield near Pärnu. Since that time we have had no information about him.

Brother Vello was arrested after grade 10 because he had not been able to hide his anti-Soviet feelings. He was released from prison camp in 1956.

Playing at the New Year's Eve party, 1952.

Brother Simmu continued his studies in Tallinn after finishing secondary school in Kuressaare and graduated from the Tallinn Polytechnic Institute. After being deported to Siberia he earned his living as an electrician and a driver.

From correspondence we found out that he had also ended up living in Krasnoyarsk territory. There he married his fellow traveler, Heljo, and they had a son.

When we learned where he was living we immediately set about trying to reunite the family. The joint decision, after discussing several options, was that Father and Mother and I would go to my brother's place, and this we did in the spring of 1953.

After returning to Estonia Simmu became an instructor and then an assistant professor at the Tallinn Polytechnic Institute. He was the best musician of the Seppel boys.

In the fall of the same year I went to Krasnoyarsk to study. The only technical university was the Siberian Institute of Forest Technology. I became a student there in the Department of Forest Engineering. Five Estonians got to study there that year: Õilme Mesila, Ipe Kabin, Rita Aire,

---

[4] This changed two years later, in 1953, after Stalin's death. [Ed.]

Juta Vilk and I. The only Estonian fellow student from the previous year was Oskar Niitepõld. Because of the studies we were in close contact with each other, especially Õilme, Ipe and I. In general the students were of many nationalities, coming both from the western and eastern regions of the USSR.

I finished three years at the institute. In the first year I lived in the main building of the institute, in a large dormitory that had beds for 24 boys. The next year I lived like a real gentleman in the newly finished men's dorm with my best Lithuanian friends, Algirdas Milašauskas and Vytautas Rakšnysega. The tight connection between our families lasts to this day. In order for the three of us to get the best living conditions, we had to work for free in the summer as auxiliary workers in construction.

Siberian Institute of Forest Technology instrumental quartet, 1954.

When the third year began, Algis and I discovered that we had not been given a place in the dorm. Vytas had become free and had gone back to Kaunas. I guess the lifestyle of our room troubled someone, so we had to find a new place to stay. We found a small room with a family of a middle-aged mother who was a teacher, and her 17-year old daughter and a son who was five years younger. For the entire year Algis and I shared a room that was about six square meters. It had a small desk, a couple of chairs and a bed suitable for a person and a half. We got along well with the host family and in the evenings were often invited for tea. The young people were especially interested in socializing with us. We were students and in addition, we were from "the west."

Doing well at the institute was usual for many of the "aliens." Most of us received higher stipends. It was sufficient so that we did not starve. Attitudes towards us were often better than they were towards the locals.

I joined several amateur musical groups, including an instrumental quartet and in the summer an orchestra that

Student field trip to the taiga.

114

played at a local resort. In addition I was invited to play at school dance parties. Back then no one could even dream of the electronic instruments that exist today. I was paid 80 to 100 rubles a night. I can say that I always had enough money to live like a student.

I also participated in sports. Vytas and I skated, and in the summer I did high jumping and he played basketball. In 1955 I was a member of the institute team and took part in the Siberian and Far East students' competitions in Tomsk.

I was also a frequent participant in other student events. In addition to those there were many events for the people from the Baltics. The most usual place for several Estonian parties was the suburban home of Karin Õunapuu (Rammulus).

In the summer of 1956 my Siberian era came to an end. When we got back to Estonia all members of our family stayed in Tallinn. We did not go back to Saaremaa. My brother Simmu and I continued our studies at the Tallinn Polytechnic Institute and graduated from there three years later. Because the curricula of the two universities didn't quite match, I had to do the third year for the second time. This allowed me to study mechanical engineering. Therefore the peak of a young person's life – student years – lasted six years for me instead of five.

At that time the Department of Mechanical Engineering at TPI was known for its high failure rate. That also applied to our group. There were 34 students but only 16 graduated on schedule. There were a couple of other peculiarities. Mechanical engineering has traditionally been a man's field, but in our group graduated the first Estonian female mechanical engineer – Olvi Särgava (Kuusik). We affectionately called her "Preili"[5] and "The First Estonian Talent."

Work as a young engineer began in the Tallinn Machine Factory, in the department of the head metallurgist; where later I became the head metallurgist. In thirteen years I had the opportunity to observe the work of Estonia's leading machine factory and to see and get acquainted with many technological processes. That was a real school of life and enriched my engineering education. That lasted until the beginning of 1972.

In 1964 Simmu approached me with the proposition for postgraduate studies. Thus began the seven-year period at the correspondence department of the Moscow Steel Institute. It was a very work-heavy period that coincided with big changes in my life. I defended my thesis on cold brittleness of cast steel. I was given the degree of the candidate of technical sciences, which opened doors to several other jobs.

One of the most important moments in the history of Estonian technology occurred when Johannes Hint won the Lenin Prize for having created the construction material silicalcite. The main idea was to crush sand grains in a disintegrator, thus giving the new material better properties. Based on this idea we developed a mutually beneficial contact, which resulted in my getting a new job at EKE Projekt. My main job was to find out how to use the disintegrator in the field of metallurgy.

In the 1970s an important turn took place in Estonian school life, starting with the widespread introduction of polytechnic education. I was invited to teach and in 1973 my teaching career began. I found a new field for myself that I liked and that matched my personality and family tradition. I was happy with my work and people were happy with me. Under different titles from senior lecturer to professor, this lasted for 34 years until I retired.

When I was in Siberia in 1953 I had met a thirteen-year-old schoolgirl by named Tiiu Siivo who along with her mother and grandmother had been sent there for her father's "crimes."

---

[5] Miss [Ed.]

Thanks to family contacts I kept track of the Siivo family from then on. Ten or so years later Tiiu had grown into a beautiful woman and was a student at the Pedagogical Institute. I was working as a young engineer at the factory. We boys from the TPI would go to their dance parties. From there developed a close friendship, falling in love, love and desire to live together, and marriage proposal with a wedding to follow on Midsummer Day of 1963. Son Avo was born to the family the next fall. At first Tiiu worked as a teacher at a secondary school and later at the TPI and the National Library.

Tiiu managed to fulfill her big dream – to establish a real Estonian country home. From her childhood she was familiar with the Pauna farm near Keila, where Tiiu's parents spent their summers. But there were two older sisters. As it happened, the sisters found new homes for themselves and offered Pauna to Tiiu and me as a country home. That took place in the spring of 1979. The old farm was in poor shape, but we were able to bring it back to life.

During summers at the farm we were occupied by field work and keeping track of the animals and birds. We had a cat and a dog, sheep, pigs, and a calf. To top it all off, in three summers we raised a total of 5,500 ducks. It was a big production. There was a lot of work but it was worth it.

In 1991 the new Estonian era began. Previous worries and activities disappeared; new ones took their place. We started a tourism farm; I became an entrepreneur.

So it went until 1998 when a disease took Tiiu from us. It had been her wish not to be separated from Pauna. Her wish was fulfilled; her ashes were scattered in the Pauna yard, and she does not have a conventional grave.

But life never stands still. A few years later Galina Valdre became the mistress of the Pauna farm. She was a widow and we had known each other for many years. Normal people have been designated to live in pairs, so we decided to join the future paths of our lives.

Galina is an architect-interior designer by profession. In the following years of our cohabitation the Pauna farmhouse became even bigger and more complete and beautiful in every way.

Galina left us on Midsummer Day of 2012.

Life in Pauna demanded constant care and work. My age kept creeping up as my strength waned. I offered the job of the master to my son Avo but he did not accept. So in 2006 we decided to sell Pauna. The Pauna period of my life lasted for 27 years.

After Estonia's re-independence many of our towns established friendship ties abroad. So did Keila. We partnered with towns in Finland, Sweden, Lithuania, Latvia and Germany. The most important for both sides was the genuine friendship with Barsbüttel, which is located near Hamburg. It began in 1992 and still continues. Contacts between the two towns are frequent and significant, from job-related and economic ties to close personal friendships. Thanks to my skills in German, I was the organizer and conductor of many excursions.

After continuously working for 57 years, I finally stopped working four years ago. My health is good for my age.

As I mentioned before, the life story of the Seppel family has been recorded in my newly published book, *Illinuku Lugu*. Happy reading!

116

Chapter 15

Aime Tootsi

I was born on 23 March 1936 at the Toomemägi Women's Clinic in the city of Tartu. The crows and jackdaws had by then already been noisily announcing the beginning of spring.

In June of 1938 my younger sister Ivi was born to the family. My two daughters and six grandchildren were also born at the Toomemägi Women's Clinic.[1]

My mother, Liisa Marie Tänna (nee Kõõra), was born in Kriimanni, Haaslava Parish, Tartu County, as the youngest of four children of a farmer's family. After attending the local school and the Girls' Grammar School of the Tartu Youth Education Society (now the Miina Härma Grammar School), she studied at the philology department of Tartu University from 1922 to 1925. Her studies were interrupted by economic reasons; farms were bought for her brothers.

My mother then graduated from the Võru Teachers' Seminary in 1926, when the principal of the seminary, Johannes Käis, led the school reform movement. Under his leadership the seminary became one of the most progressive establishments in Estonia. In her work as a teacher, Liisa Tänna also followed the progressive principles of Johannes Käis. From 1926 to 1944 Mother worked as a teacher at the Kuldre School in Võru County. During that time she was an active member of Women's Home Defense. On 24 February 1938[2] Liisa Tänna was awarded the Cross of the Order of the Eagle Class V and the Women's Defense White Cross.

One year old, with Mother.

My father, Aleksander Tänna, was born in the town of Valga[3] to the family of a railroad worker with four children. Father graduated from the local school and worked in several

---

[1] The clinic is now the Department of Social Services of the University of Tartu. [Ed.]
[2] Estonian Independence Day is 24 February. [Ed.]
[3] Valga is on the Latvian border in southern Estonia. On the other side of the border is the Latvian town of Valka. Today there are not fences or border crossings between the two towns. [Ed.]

fields, such as rafting logs on the Koiva River, and later in Valga as a conductor, a hand-car driver on the railroad, and in other jobs. He also acquired the profession of a driver, and because he was living in a border town, spoke fluent Latvian.

Ivi and I with relatives, end of summer, 1948 in Äksi.

We lived in the Kuldre schoolhouse, which was built in 1910. It was quite a modern building for its time – a two-story construction of red brick. The first floor included accommodations for the principal, teacher and the school maid. A staircase in the vestibule led to the second floor where the classrooms and the school assembly hall were located. My childhood passed in the milieu of the school; everyday life went in the same rhythm as school life, always surrounded by many children and activities. I recall Christmas parties, common games in the schoolyard, and the springtime end-of-school hikes to the Uhtjärv in Urvaste, and much more.

My education also began in Kuldre School, in 1943. The school year was cut short because of the war. In the spring of 1944 the schoolhouse became headquarters for the retreating German army. The schoolyard filled with war machines, and the schoolhouse was occupied by German soldiers. Russian planes were now and then diving and strafing. I remember that the children were told that, if they were caught outside during an air raid, they should lie down on their stomachs.

In the middle of August 1944 war reached Võrumaa. When we heard the echoes of war from the Antsla direction, the evacuations began. We managed to get on a German army truck headed for Tartu. The Germans wanted to take us on a train headed for Germany, but Mother didn't agree to that. So they left us at the side of the road. A kind local horse-driver who was passing by took us with him, and we spent the night at his place. The next morning he took us to the Puka station to catch a train. We finally reached our grandparents and other relatives in the Äksi area near Saadjärv in Tartu County.

A few weeks later the battles between the advancing Red Army and the German rear guard started in the Tartu vicinity. We decided to hide in a remote place, away from large roads, in the Kiisa farm belonging to Mother's sister. The farm was on the edge of a small swamp by the railway. Thus we hoped to be left out of the vortex of battle. In the cattle kitchen of the barn, which had thick natural stone walls, were other refugees from the city of Tartu. Suddenly German tanks entered the yard, and the battle began with the Russians who were in the swamp behind the barn. We were caught in the middle of the battle and had to escape quickly. With Mother and Sister we crawled behind the railway hedge. Bullets flew over our heads. Mother said, "Don't be afraid, it's the phone lines that are making that sound!"

Looking back, we saw a big pillar of smoke over the farm. Later we learned that an old barn had caught fire and burned down.

In Voldi (Tabivere railway station) there was a train with empty cattle cars. German soldiers were calmly washing themselves at the well. We found out that the train would be

118

heading back towards Tallinn. We managed to find a corner for ourselves on the floor of a cattle car. Later we found out that we had been near Pupartvere Village where the Finnish Boys had fought a gallant battle against the Red Army. The Finnish Boys had arrived in Volt on the same train we were now taking. Because of their resistance, the entire Tartu front was stalled. Today, in Äksi next to the Ice Age Museum, is an interesting Finnish Boys' Museum-Room with many exhibits.

We arrived in Tallinn barefoot and empty-handed, just as we had fled. We were taken in by relatives in Pääsküla, on the edge of a marsh in a private residence on Kadaka Alley. There were bunk beds built in the basement of the house where people slept at night. Other relatives had gathered here as well. I walked to the Nõmme market to buy food when it was available. Several days at the end of September were hectic for Estonia but somehow quiet in Pääsküla. From time to time we heard explosions at a distance. I recall older people talking about how the blue-black-and-white flag had been seen flying on top of Tall Hermann.[4] That seemed unbelievable to everyone back then. No one knew what would happen in the future.

And so the Soviets arrived on 22 September 1944. Two soldiers with red stars on their hats and rifles with bayonets entered the garden gate and the house through two different doors. The house was searched; the bayonets were stuck under the beds and behind corners. We kids were supposed to hide in the basement because there were rumors that something could happen to children, but instead we practically ran into the soldiers. Luckily, they were not interested in children, but they were checking for German soldiers. On their departure they took some small items that had caught their attention.

Father, who had been looking for us amidst the chaos, arrived in Tallinn and thus we decided to stay in Tallinn. We managed to find accommodations in an apartment on Kalev Street.

Schools opened again at the end of October or beginning of November 1944. Our nearest school was on Vabrik Street and I entered second grade. In those days boys and girls were in separate classes. The school was then called Tallinn Incomplete Secondary School No. 15 (now Kalamaja Public School). Russian school classes began in the same buildings as a second shift. Life went on.

Sister Ivi and I made friends among the neighborhood children. I became good friends with Eve, whose friendship lasts to this day. Our playground was a green park, young trees and snowball bushes, established in the days of the Estonian Republic. Today this is the Salme Cultural Center. At school we played ring games during breaks, and there were parties and performances at the school assemblies. I was a good student and also became a Pioneer.[5] As a part of our activities, we were sent to clean up the city streets of demolition debris from destroyed buildings. We carried stones and rubble on stretchers to the school. There were rumors of "sausage mills" in the ruins.

During the complicated post-war days, I decided to learn to play the piano. Mother found both a piano teacher and a piano. Eve and I started taking piano classes at Niine Street. Years later Eve graduated from the Tallinn Conservatory as a pianist. For me, this skill came in

---

[4] Tall Hermann is one of the corner towers of the Old Town of Tallinn, and the flag flying from the tower is a symbol of a free Estonian nation. [Ed.]

[5] The Pioneer youth organization was run by the Communist Party. Pioneering replaced Boy Scouts and Girl Scouts, which were disbanded by the communists because the communists considered them to be fascist organizations. [Ed.]

handy during my years in Siberia when I was, at age 13, invited to work as a pianist at the kindergarten.

After the war Mother got a job as an Estonian language teacher at the Tallinn Secondary School No. 1[6], and Father got a job as a driver at the railroad office. Secondary School No. 1 was then a boys' school. Ivi and I often waited at the gate of the school for Mother to come from work.

On one November day in 1945 we were waiting for Father to come home from work. He didn't come. In January 1946 the decision of the Railway Tribunal came: §58 (pg. 1a, 11, and 10+5).[7]

Food was short in Tallinn after the war. The farmers' market was between the Estonia Theater and Musumägi. We also received food from grandparents in Tartumaa – groats, flour, and beet syrup. We naturally also queued for sugar like everyone back then.

The summer holidays we would spend in Äksi with our grandparents and Mother's older brother's family who had a farm. Mother had to participate in many summer courses.

At the farm our family playmates of our ages, Aime and Ilme, were growing. The steady and calm everyday rhythm of the farm life, children's participation in the farm work according to their abilities, animals, closeness to nature, and the love of grandparents gave us, the children, a sense of security so necessary in those complicated times. These summers were the most beautiful times of my childhood.

In 1946 I attended seventh grade at the local school in Kukulinna.

In 1949, when I celebrated my thirteenth birthday, I received several nice books as birthday gifts. I planned to read these books during the summer, but that year we never made it to the Tartumaa farm.

Late in the evening of 24 March 1949 Mother came home from the Marxism-Leninism lectures that were mandatory for teachers. That night there was a demanding knock on the door. Younger sister Ivi had climbed in bed with Mother and was thinking that it must be burglars. Mother didn't open the door. Some time later the house manager's voice said, "Mrs. Tänna, open the door!" Then Mother woke me up, too. There were already many people in the rooms, and there was an armed guard at the door. I couldn't understand why we had to get dressed and start going someplace in Siberia. A stranger was reading something to us from a paper. Two women among the strangers started sewing big bags of our two bedcovers on our sewing machine. Clothes from our wardrobe were then tossed into these bags, along with the sewing machine. There was a truck with a gunman in front of the house. The windows in our house were dark, but we could see the curtains quietly waving "farewell."

On our journey through the night we saw trucks in front of some other houses as well. At the station was a train with cattle cars with bars on the windows. More and more people were brought in. There were two-level bunk beds in the car. The children had to climb into the high bunks right below the ceiling. Older people were lying on their bags under the bunks. When the car was full, the doors were closed. People were somehow trying to get letters and notices out from between the bars and closed window shutters. It later turned out that our letter did reach our folks in Tartumaa.

I think it was Ülemiste station where the train stopped for several days. How we managed in the sealed cars of the train, I do not recall. I remember that we tried hard to see through

---

[6] Now the Gustav Adolf Grammar School. [Ed.]
[7] His sentence was ten years in prison plus five years in exile.[Ed.]

the cracks in the window shutters, to see from our high bunks what was going on outside. After several days the train started to move. The people in the car were quiet and in tears.

In the middle of the car were toilet buckets where needs could be taken care of while people sheltered each other. When the train started, the buckets spilled over. At each stop the people had to bang on the doors to get the guards to open up so that the buckets could be emptied.

There was also a cast iron stove (*burzhuika*) in the car. People took turns warming themselves when coal or other fuel was found. At night the stove went out and the walls were covered with white frost.

On the journey the train sometimes stood for a long time on a siding. We met similar cattle car trains with Latvians, Lithuanians, and Ukrainians. In the bigger stations representatives of the cars were given buckets to fetch boiled soup and millet. We traveled through the cities of Vologda, Molotov, Sverdlovsk, and over the Urals. From there on the car doors were open. Western Siberia seemed flat, empty and scary looking.

On an early morning in April when we had arrived at the Atchinsk station on the Siberian railway, we had to exit the car with our bags and possessions. It was cold. We found out that our exile was to last forever. Forever – that destroyed all hope of returning to Estonia. Adults had to sign the papers and to turn in their passports. There was a 25-year jail sentence for attempted escape. We spent the night on the floor of the Atchinsk railway station.

Next day we were taken from Atchinsk on a truck 40-50 kilometers away to the district center in Bolshoi-Ului, located on the high bank of the Tchulym River, an Ob River tributary. Representatives of local collective farms with their horses and sleighs had been sent here. The so-called "slave market" took place. It was by chance that people found jobs and housing. Everyone was confused. We were to be taken 4 to 5 kilometers into the *taiga* to the village of Klimovka. But first we had to cross the Tchulym River on which the ice had started to break. Children and bags were put on sleighs while the adults walked alongside, often knee-deep in ice water.

We arrived at a typical Siberian Russian village. Along the long, muddy road were log houses with carved wood decorations on the windows. Each house had a small garden by the front window with a bench for sitting in front of each yard. Behind the houses were vegetable and potato beds, and all around was the *taiga*. In a separate building in the village was a four-grade school.

All the deportees were housed with the locals. The three of us and another mother with her son were accommodated on the kitchen floor of a small house. A few days later we had to move to another house that had more room; at least there were two living rooms. In a corner of one of the rooms the three of us were given a cot for sleeping. The room had a typical Russian oven with a sleeping space on the oven. The floors were of wood. Every Saturday we cleaned them according to the local custom by either scraping with a knife or by rubbing with a broom and sand to make them white again. We were in a collective farm by the name of *Vtoraja Bolschevistskaya Vesna*. [8]

The deportees were initially sent to work in the forest. Every person had to cut and stack four cubic meters of wood a day. That was counted as the quota. The city people didn't have the clothing or footwear to work in the forest in the early spring thaw, and the walk to the forest was 4 to 5 kilometers of a practically non-existent road.

---

[8] Second Bolshevik Spring. [Ed.]

The collective farmers' cows, with bells around their necks, went on their own to the pasture every morning and came back home in the evening. The foreman rode on his horse through the village in the morning, knocked on all the windows and announced who would be working where and on what.

The deportees were initially given prepayment of a few kilograms of flour and some milk processed through the cattle barn. We children would fetch that from the milk kiosk. We had to climb over the cattle fences and were scared of the big bull. Those people who wanted land to plant small vegetable gardens were given the land.

We had serious problems with food. We were trading our things for potatoes. Our relatives and some good friends from Estonia supported us as much as they could. My dear schoolmates in Estonia sent us letters and newspapers. That was all great support back in those days. We had not been forgotten.

At first the local children chased us, laughing at us. We had to hear the word "fascist." Eventually we began to play together and enjoyed common activities and games like softball. We went bathing in the river, and once in the *taiga* at a beekeeper's house we ate fresh cucumbers with honey. A trip to the apiary every summer was a tradition in the village.

On weekdays children were sent to the collective farm fields to pick thistles. The fields were next to the *taiga* forests, and in summer mosquitoes, horseflies and *moshka*[9] bothered us. One had to wear airtight clothes. The local children smeared some kind of black and stinky birch tar on their faces and necks. We tried this as well. We put thick netting in front of our faces as defense against the mosquitoes and the *moshka*.

The Tchulym River had a lot of fish. We went with Mother to "lift out" the fish from the high bank of the river with a net. The fish were small but still a welcome addition to our food table. Sometimes we also fished with rods for bigger fish. We built a smoking fire on the shore to protect against mosquitoes and *moshka*. It was exciting.

Thanks to her well-wishing colleagues, Mother was sent her vacation pay from her school in Tallinn. We, along with an Estonian married couple, bought a cow. The cow spent three days in our family and three days in theirs. I can't imagine how we were able to feed the cow through the winter.

In August a group of Estonians were to be relocated to an industrial area. Mother was very worried about our education. She was hoping that the industrial area would provide us a greater chance to go to school. We were lucky and got on the list. When we departed, the cow simply stayed with the other family as they did not have the money to pay us for our share.

In the middle of September of 1949 began the trip from the collective farm to the Bolshoi-Ului district center. At first we used horses and carts, but then we continued the trip in a truck, to Atchinsk. Then we were taken by convoy to a deportation camp in the suburb of Krasnoyarsk.

The camp consisted of fenced-in barracks. The territory was guarded by gunmen. Only children could exit. We went to the surrounding houses to trade our belongings for potatoes and large onions. We would bake those in the ashes of the oven of our room. We had two-story bunk beds for sleeping. I don't recall any kind of washing options. People of many nationalities – men and women – went through that camp. Everyone came from somewhere and went again.

---

[9] Black flies. [Ed.]

There was, however, a possibility for families to reunite. Recruiters would also come here to recruit workers for construction, mining, and factory work in new industrial areas in the north. The more able bodied and younger were always selected. The available "slaves" were all lined up and the recruiters would select those they found suitable.

Older people and women with children stayed in that camp for a longer period. Only towards the end of October the remaining Estonians (we among them) were taken 50 kilometers from Krasnoyarsk to the industrial settlement of a glass factory by the name of Pamyati 13-i Bortsov[10] in the Yemelyanovo district, located on the slopes of the valley of the Kaatcha River, a rapidly-flowing tributary of the Yenissei River. A beautiful pine forest grew on the slopes.

The settlement had been named in memory of thirteen fallen soldiers in the battle against the White Army. A monument had been erected for them on the mountain slope. During the May and October festivities people would gather there and hold meetings.

Moving there was great luck for us! The settlement had a secondary school, two kindergartens, hospital, pharmacy, public sauna, store, clubhouse, and so on. We were given a room in barracks where the only heat was a flue from the stove in the next room.

When we arrived snow was already on the ground. The houses looked as if they were dug into the ground, and that was what they were. In the fall soil would be piled up to the windows and dug out again in the spring. Winter was on its way and we needed heat to survive. We lived and slept on top of our clothes bags. From the firewood storage bin at the factory we occasionally got some firewood, a sleighful at a time. In the spring we would collect pine cones for heating. We brought water with a yoke from a deep well on the slope of the mountain.

Ivi and I got to go to school. The schoolhouse was a two-story, thin-walled wood building. I dropped back to grade 5, and Ivi to grade 3. Mother figured it would be easier for us in the lower grades. Since the material was familiar to us we would initially simply memorize specific paragraphs of the narrative subjects.

Writing in Russian was more complicated. I remember my first written re-telling of the story "Strelotchnik." [11] I sort of understood something of the content, and the Russian boy sitting next to me tried to help and correct me. The result in the end was more red pencil than anything else. Teachers and fellow students were generally kind to us. By spring of 1950 the biggest worries were over. There were no real problems in other subjects. By the end of the school year we started to settle into school life.

In December of 1949 I was invited to play the piano at the kindergartens. I learned Russian children's songs and often accompanied the teachers on the piano in singing to the children. I was paid more than Mother who at the time had to work at the glass factory. Her job was picking up pieces of glass for which she received minimum pay.

The year-end parties at the kindergartens were memorable. The decorated fir tree and the children in costumes were enjoyable. I stayed to work at the kindergarten for all the years I was going to school. In summers I did the same job. My working allowed us to somehow manage our lives.

Because all the kindergarten activities took place in the morning, I had to do my own studying in the evening. The only light in the classroom during that time was an oil lamp on

---

[10] Memory of Thirteen Fighters. [Ed.]
[11] "Pointman." [Ed.]

the teacher's desk. The hallway was quite dark. Despite everything, I attended grade 7 in a regular school.

In 1952 when I had turned 16 I received a notice from the local commandant that I had to show up there to be accounted for as a deportee (as a *spetspereselenka*). I ignored the first notice because I thought the request was unfair. The second notice was already threatening – if I did not show, a gunman would be sent for me. The procedure was demeaning to me. A form was filled out with my personal information – eye color, height, surgery scars, Adam's apple, and so on. I had to answer several kinds of questions. Now I also had to start going to the commandant to give my signature every month. In addition I had to sign a paper that said I understood that if I tried to escape, I would go to prison for 25 years.

People of many nationalities lived at the settlement: Germans from Volga and Odessa, Kalmyks, Lithuanians, Tatars, Jews, Ukrainians, some Latvians, and former Russian White Army soldiers.

The day started with a hooting whistle of the factory at seven o'clock in the morning. In those days the glass factory manufactured lamp chimneys, bottles, and glass containers of a specific shape (so-called *krõnkas*). These were used by the locals for storing milk. Once the glass containers were washed, they were put upside down on fence posts to dry. Fairly frequently the factory was not working due to shortages of raw material or heating fuel. Then everyone was sent to the forest to gather wood.

The factory whistle also hooted when a berry gatherer had got lost in the *taiga* and people were called to look for the missing person. The whistle also hooted for large *taiga* fires, when a bitter layer of smoke floated over the settlement. When there was a *taiga* fire, people would gather with axes and shovels and ride into the woods to put out the fire.

Berry picking in the *taiga* was done in groups with a few older women who knew the *taiga* and berry locations. Not everyone was allowed to go. Wild red and black currant shrubs grew in the *taiga*, as well as raspberries. Big and sweet bird cherries were also picked. These were dried and milled, and then used for baking pies.

Ivi, Mother and I at our new living quarters, 1952.

We would also go into the *taiga* with a group of children to pick cedar cones. In the spring, the *taiga* was full of blooms and colorful wild peonies, globeflowers ("ogonki"),[12] violets, and Siberian irises. The globeflowers were bigger and much more orange in color than our dear golden Estonian ones.

Ivi and I attended

---

[12] *Kullerkupp* in Estonian. [Ed.]

124

school; we had a lot to do and many friends. In spring when the bird cherries were in bloom, the *karmoshka*[13] would call us together with the other youths to the summer garden for a dance. High emotions and a hope for a bright future were shared by all of us young people.

Now, reading Mother's letters written to the folks back home, I am beginning to understand what she went through and how worried she was. She would stand all night in queues for bread, and even then often did not get any. But the force to survive would always win.

A few years later we were given the oppor-tunity to move to other barracks, with a small room on the first floor where a stove with a flue had been built. We thus got away from the constant cold and the snow blowing into our room. Here our neighbor behind a thin board wall was a calf. A newborn calf would be brought into the room to wait for warmer weather to go outside, and it would sweetly click its little hooves right behind the wall by my sleeping cot.

Many young, highly educated, and good teachers worked at the school. The math teacher was a strict man who always wore a soldier's coat. He always gave us many problems to solve in class. I liked that, and I found it interesting. Our history teacher was also our homeroom teacher.

When Stalin died in 1953 there was a mourning of several days at school. The homeroom teacher had to interrupt the lesson and leave the classroom several times in tears.

Ivi and I in dresses Mother sewed for us, 1952.

In the fall the school would send us to nearby collective farms to pick potatoes and do other harvest work. The boys would dig up the ground with hoes (as they felt like it) and the girls picked the potatoes. Much was left in the ground and not picked.

A remarkable event for our family took place in the spring of 1954. We received a note from Mother's sister Ida, who was traveling through Krasnoyarsk. She was looking for the grave of her husband, who had died in the Taishet prison camp. Aunt Ida carried in her heart the wish to say a prayer on her husband's grave, and to collect three handfuls of the Siberian soil to take in a small bag to the family burial plot at the Äksi cemetery. On her way back she promised to visit with us. We were looking forward to it, but in the next two weeks we received no more word from her. We learned later that she had fallen ill on her way back and had been rushed back home. Our disappointment was of course great, but she had succeeded in her brave quest.

When Mother was later working as a gardener at the hospital, we helped her weed and water the beds. We covered the cucumber beds in the evening to protect them from cold and uncovered them again in the morning. We also had a potato field and a vegetable garden. We used a shovel to plant the potatoes just as the locals did. We carried the potato buckets to

---

[13] Accordion. [Ed.]

the field and back home with yokes. The earth had to be turned with a shovel. The soil was rich and if one was eager to weed and hoe, one could expect a nice crop, depending on the summer. The local variety of potato, the so-called *kulturka*,[14] produced enormous potatoes in a good year. To plant, a large potato would be cut in pieces, each piece with four to five eyes. During our last year there Mother also got a piglet.

In winter, Mother worked at the hospital, initially as the night guard, the central heat person, and later as the orderly, laundry person, cook, nurse-hostess, and so on. In 1953 there was an outbreak of typhoid in the surrounding areas, and typhoid patients from elsewhere were brought to this hospital. At that particular time Mother was working in the hospital laundry, where the bed linens were done by hand.

Mother fell ill with typhoid because disinfectants were practically non-existent. For some time she was quarantined. Every day we went to see her through the hospital window. She was lying almost a week without moving, with her eyes closed. Luckily Mother got better after a long and serious illness, and neither Ivi nor I got sick.

Secondary school graduate, 1955.

At home we would speak Estonian with each other. But there were few other Estonians, so we became more and more assimilated into the local environment, locals' customs, and traditions. We felt no different from the locals.

When the loudspeakers sometimes played a song by Estonian singer Georg Ots, Mother always called out to us, "Come and listen. Georg Ots is calling us back home!"

In 1955 Father, who had been set free from prison and had been given permission to reunite with his family, joined us.

In 1955 I graduated from the local secondary school with the silver medal and started my studies at the Krasnoyarsk Pedagogical Institute in the Department of Mathematics. That was the first year that deportees were accepted at that school. The pedagogical institute was located on the main street of Krasnoyarsk, Stalin Prospect.

At seven o'clock in the morning of 2 September all first-year students were sent from the river port on a ferry along the Yenissei River to a grain harvest at the Novosyolovo district. The journey lasted two days and nights. We were housed in a small village in the middle of the steppe. The only wooden construction was a relatively thin-walled so-called club house that became our home for two long months. The village houses were clay huts with soil roofs. Grass grew on the roofs, and the huts had dirt floors. The grain fields sprawled away from the village. The harvested grain was piled in an empty field in large piles called windrows.

We girls loaded grain onto seven-ton trucks with big shovels. This work continued through the night shift. We also had to shovel the grain from one pile to another so that it would not heat up. Later we would clean the seed grain with a winnower, also on the night shift. When we carried the grain buckets to pour them into the winnower, we would observe the starry

---

[14] Cultured. [Ed.]

sky and recite poetry by Yessenin.[15] When we got cold we would climb into the hot grain to warm up. We would come out of it all damp and we would soon be cold again. But still, it was pleasant to be warm for a while.

We got back to Krasnoyarsk for the October holidays, with our clothes and footwear worn through.

Two other Estonian girls with whom we became acquainted also came to study at the pedagogical institute that fall – Leida Niitepõld and Evi Pilt. Through Leida I met her brother Oskar Niitepõld and other Estonians who at the time were studying at the Siberian Institute of Forest Technology in Krasnoyarsk.

With Ivi, Oskar and Leida at my place in Krasnoyarsk.

We were already acquainted with Dagi and Peedu Treikelder, who also lived in Krasnoyarsk. After leaving the glass factory, Dagi had married Leo Lipre. We visited them a few times at their home.

These contacts allowed us to join the Estonian community in Krasnoyarsk. I recall common Christmases, meetings with Oskar and Leida, with Rein Saluvere, Allan Onton, Kaljo Käspre, Ants Lond and others. I became friends with Maie Lond, who, after marrying Märt Lond, had moved to Krasnoyarsk and lived near me. Maie sometimes invited Ivi and me to keep her company when Märt was on a work trip.

Thanks to Mother's contacts in the hospital, I had found accommodations with a Jewish lady, a former doctor on Karl Marx Street, quite close to the institute. Of the Krasnoyarsk days I remember the powerful cracking and rumbling of ice on the Yenissei River when the ice was breaking up. The entire city would rush to the river bank to admire the sight.

In 1956 the construction of a new bridge over the Yenissei River started in Krasnoyarsk. As students

In the front, Peet with accordion, me, Ivi, ?, Dagi's mother, and in the back, Leo and Dagi.

---

[15] Sergei Yessenin (1895 - 1925) was one of the most famous Russian poets of the 20th century. [Ed.]

we were sent there a few times to assist in the work, especially when the river was covered with ice.

In the second year at the institute, in the fall of 1956, we again had to go to the collective farm, this time for only three weeks – to the Daursk district of Krasnoyarsk Krai. We mostly worked at the drier and other harvesting works. For our labors we each earned two bags of grain, which the locals were happy to buy from us. The military had also been brought in to participate in the harvest. Soldiers carried the grain to the big truck trains.

One day in the beginning of October 1956 a special event was in store for me; the dean of the department personally came to tell me that, according to a notice received from the commandant, I had to appear there to arrange for documents for my freedom.

The commandant asked about my plans for the future. I was given a certificate with which I could now be a free person and apply for a passport. I heard that Mother and Father were also offered their freedom. To apply for a passport I had to translate my birth certificate from Estonian to Russian and then have it notarized in the presence of another Estonian speaker. Peet Treikelder, with whom I went to the notary, signed for the correctness of the translation.

Now I had to save money for the trip back. Ivi was in the last year of secondary school, and I was in the second year of the institute. We planned our return trip home for the summer of 1957.

Because I was living in the city, it became my job to get the train tickets home. At the same time, the summer of 1957, an international youth festival was taking place in Moscow, and the tickets for the Moscow train were extremely difficult to obtain.

At the Krasnoyarsk train station. I am second from left. To my left is Father. Far right is Ivi.

To get the tickets one had to queue up at the station box office, receive a queue number and, after the box office was closed, at an agreed on time on several occasions gather at the station yard for "pereklitchka."[16] If some-one was not there, his or her number was given to the next person. That's how one advanced in numbers. When the number of tickets was equal to the number of people in the queue, the tickets were sold.

It worked! On the morning of the third day I was at the front of the line and received four tickets for the Moscow train.

---

[16] Roll call. [Ed.]

Mother and Father had taken care of packing our belongings and had made the other preparations for the trip home. Filled with anticipation, we began our journey home on 11 July 1957.

We were back home on Estonian soil on 15 July 1957, getting off the Moscow-Tallinn train at the Tartu station. We had dreamed about this moment, hoped and waited for it. But now that we were here, how could we manage? What was waiting for us?

On the train we had met Leida Niitepõld's younger brother Jaan Niitepõld, who was traveling to take the admission exams to the Tallinn Maritime School so as to become a captain. (He was successful.) He commemorated our arrival in Tartu in a photo.

The joy of the reunion with Grandmother and other relatives, who were waiting for us, was great, although Grandmother was clearly ill. It was a wonderful feeling to hear Estonian spoken around us and to see people dear and familiar to us. We had carried memories of them in our minds all the years we had spent away. How nice that everyone was still there.

Welcome at Tartu. Aime and Ivi with their mother and father.

But they had also changed, just as we had changed. What followed was a time of rearranging life, getting used to new conditions, and taking time to rediscover oneself. A big thanks to all those who supported us then!

I continued my studies at the Tallinn Pedagogical Institute, named after Eduard Vilde, at the third year of the Department of Mathematics-Physics. I joined the Russian language study group because I considered my expressive skills in Estonian insufficient. That was the last Russian language group in the institute, however, and in the spring semester I transferred to the Estonian group. Having got a space at the newly opened dorm on Lomonossov Street, by January of 1958 I soon felt at home again in Tallinn. I graduated from the institute in 1960.

For two years I worked in Tartumaa at the Reola eight-grade school as a teacher. The school later became Ülenurme Grammar School.

In 1961 I married Rein Tootsi, and in 1962 we got jobs and accommodations at the Tõravere Observatory. Although the main building and residential houses were still under construction, we still hoped to get an apartment there. When the institute moved to Tartu, I got a job at the institute's mathematics lab. In 1971 the Tõravere department of the self-sustaining Programming Office under the Academy of Sciences Institute of Cybernetics was formed, and I continued working there. The last four years before my retirement I worked with the observatory work group on theoretical astrophysics.

Daughters Tiiu and Anu were born. My mother lived with us in Tõravere, but she became ill with rheumatoid arthritis and left us forever in 1977. Father had died in 1965 as a result of his third heart attack. They are both resting in Tartu Raadi (Maarja) Cemetery.

I have had the good fortune to live, work and to associate with wonderful people during the Tõravere times and to be a part of its rich spirit.

My husband and I are retired now, and we cheer on our children's and grandchildren's activities and lives. Almost every year we meet with the Estonians who from 1953 to 1957 studied in the higher education establishments of Krasnoyarsk. We are joined by the common memories of our youth in Siberia.

I am grateful to all the good people and fellow travelers who have been a part of my life and who have defined who I am.

I have written this story so that the next generations that grow up in free Estonia remember the past and be able to value the freedom they have been given. I conclude with the words that President Lennart Meri said to me during the ceremony of "Estonia Remembers" at the Elva song festival ground on 8 July 2001: "We're still alive, Mrs. Tootsi!"

Chapter 16

Ivi Peekmann

My story is of course similar to the story of my sister Aime.

I will start my story from the time when in the late fall of 1949 we (myself, Mother and sister Aime) arrived in Siberia at the Posyolok pamyati 13-i Bortsov settlement of the Yemelyanovo district where Mother got her first job as a transportation worker. Aime and I went to school. Instead of the fifth grade I went to the third. The elementary school building was a small low building located on the slope of the mountain. The secondary school that my sister was attending was two stories high and closer to our home. How I managed with Russian I don't quite remember, but I finished grade 4 with a letter of commendation.

The next years followed in most part like this: in winters, studies and skiing; in summers, bathing in the Kaatcha river, berry picking in the *taiga*, and gathering cedar cones. My first skis were made for me of birch by Uncle Nugis, who had also been deported and lived in the same house with us. He also installed the bindings on my *valenki*. Later, in secondary school, I took part in the district skiing competitions and achieved the second level in youth skiing.

In 1954 I finished grade 7. With Mother's approval I decided to continue my studies at the Krasnoyarsk Mining Technical School. I passed the admission exams but I was not admitted. The reason was that I had been deported and the field of mining required me to spend time in restricted areas. I remember that twin brothers, Volga Germans by nationality, received very good marks on their admission exams but they, too, were not admitted. I heard that they were not happy with that and sought assistance from an attorney. Now in hindsight I cannot remember if I had my passport at the time or not.

I know for sure that I received my passport in the summer of 1954 when I turned 16. People born in 1938 were not accounted for at the commandant's office. I went to the district center militia station to receive the passport. I did not have a birth certificate. Mother gave me a document that had been issued to her by Urvaste Parish regarding the number of children in the family. I translated this for the officials. It said that a daughter Ivi had been born 19 June 1938, and that's how I received the passport. The name on the passport was Тянна Ива Александровна (Tyanna Iva Alesandrovna) and that's who I was until 1960 when I got married.

With classmates, 1955.

I continued my studies in the old school, grade 8. Grades 8, 9, 10 were considered secondary school.

Sister Aime graduated from secondary school in 1955 and continued her studies at the Krasnoyarsk Pedagogical Institute. I missed my sister and visited her every chance I got. From the settlement to the city 50 kilometers away, one could travel on an open truck with benches. At my sister's I, too, met the other Estonians in Krasnoyarsk and joined their community. They were for the most part young and the majority of them were studying at the forestry institute. In her story Aime writes more about the people in our circle.

In June of 1957 I graduated from secondary school. By then our family had been reunited as Father had arrived in 1955. He had been set free from prison and given permission to join the family.

The trip home to Estonia was planned for July. I decided to continue my studies at the Leningrad Railway Institute in the field of electrical engineering, where I sent my documents right after finishing secondary school.

We arived in Estonia on 15 July 1957 when we stepped off the Moscow-Tallinn train in Tartu. It was a great joy to see Grandmother again. She had been eagerly waiting for us!

Very soon after that I had to travel to Leningrad to take the admission exams to the Railway Institute. I shared a dorm room on Malaya Posadskaya Street with three girls. Exams were in five subjects. To get the maximum 25 points, one had to get "five" for each exam. I was the only one in our dorm room who had chosen the field of electrical engineering; the others were going to study energetics, bridges, tunnels, and traffic.

I received 23 points for the five exams but I was not on the list of admitted students. There was a note at the bottom of the list that I had to come to the institute the next morning. A six-member committee questioned me. It turned out that I had not been referred to study by the Soviet Republic and they could not admit me because of that. The girls in my room passed the exams with 15 points. I took my exam transcript and left.

Once I arrived in Estonia, I went to Pärnu to the home of Father's sister Aunt Lilli. She had come to visit me in Leningrad during the exams and also supported me financially. I was planning to go to work. September had already started. However, I then received word from Mother in Tartu that Tartu Rail Transportation Technical School had announced an additional admission for secondary school graduates. Mother recommended not to lose any more time on studies. On 10 September 1957 I presented my exam transcript and application to the principal Peilman. I was immediately accepted to the rail traffic field with the study term of 2.5 years. All the other technical school students had already been sent to collective farms, but I was held behind and told to sort out the library. I also got a spot in the Kooli Street dormitory.

For the first two months I was in a Russian study group, as I felt I could not manage in Estonian. Evi Kikas, who had just returned from Siberia, joined me. Later we both joined the Estonian group.

I graduated from the technical school in 1960 with commendation (the so-called diploma with red covers). Once again the opportunity presented itself to study at the Leningrad

Railway Transportation Institute without admission exams. Unfortunately I had to give up that idea due to economic reasons. My sister and I were both practically living off scholarships. We were young and at the beginning of our lives.

Trained station managers organize and are responsible for the safe movement of trains in the station and in the adjacent areas. From 1960 to 1974 I worked as the station manager at several stations: Riisipere, Klooga, Saue, Nõmme, Lagedi. Now some of these stations have been closed.

In 1960 I married Jüri Enn Peekmann. Jüri Enn also worked for the railroad, at the car depot as an electrician. We were given an apartment in a new house to be built in Tallinn. Our sons Vaido and Raivo were born.

In 1965 the Leningrad Railway Transportation Institute opened a study-consultation office in Tallinn in the rooms of the old conductors' school (now the Swedish consulate). It was meant for rail workers who wanted to participate in distance learning. Lectures took place one day a week; lab work was done at the TPI. I once more used the opportunity to study and got admitted to the distance study program. I finished the first two years in Tallinn. In the third year I had to travel often between Tallin and Leningrad (exam sessions and such) and to stay there as well for extended periods. This got to be too much. I had to decide in favor of home and the children.

In 1973 daughter Ene was born to the family.

In 1974 I was invited to work at the Railway Office (36 Pikk Street) as a train dispatcher. I mostly worked in the Tallinn-Tapa area. In that area the train traffic took place according to a fully automated blocking system, and traffic was controlled remotely from Pikk Street. We were in touch by radio transmitters with the train conductors. Traffic graphs needed to be drawn, and railway routing was determined on such analyses. I also worked on the Tartu-Valga-Petseri, Tallinn-Haapsalu-Paldiski lines. The last diesel train departed from Tallinn to Haapsalu in 1995.

Work on the railway took place in four shifts. Because the job of a train dispatcher was considered hazardous, I had the opportunity to retire at 50 (in 1988). I continued working as a pensioner.

My husband Jüri Enn passed away in 1989. I later married my coworker Leo Jõgisoo. The free time of our life together was mostly spent fixing up Leo's father's farm and garden in Jäneda. In 2003, at the age of 65, I finally quit going to work. Leo passed away in July of 2007.

My three children all live in Tallinn. I'm a grandmother to five grandchildren.

Perhaps I was too self-centered writing this story. But my memories of my mother, grandmother, and good relatives are indelible.

Meetings with the former Siberia-companions connect us to the past and the present. To my dearest journey companion – my sister – I always say, "We're still alive!"

Epilog

It has now been 65 years since the 1949 deportations.

On 14 June 2014 - on a national day of mourning - Estonia's President Toomas Hendrik Ilves invited the survivors of the 1949 deportations to his official residence in Kadriorg and met with them in the rose garden. The authors of the original Estonian version of this book, all survivors of the deportation, presented a copy of the book to the President. The book was compiled and edited by Rita Metsis.

Rita Metsis presenting their book, *Unustamatud Noorusaastad Siberis* **to President T. H. Ilves.**

With the President in the rose garden are co-authors Ants Lond, Malle Vesilind, and Rita Metsis.

135